Echoes of the Ancient World
Series editor Werner Forman

THE MOORS

THE MOORS
ISLAM IN THE WEST

Text by Michael Brett
Photographs by Werner Forman

GOLDEN

For Annabel

As if the river spread a parchment,
whose lines were written by the gentle breeze,
Above the page appearing on the surface,
bent down to read the branches of the trees.

Ibn Sa'id, Las Banderas, 66

Front endpaper: The Muslim West in the tenth century AD

Back endpaper: The Muslim West between the eleventh and thirteenth centuries AD

Half-title page: Seated musician: a detail from an ivory panel of
the Fatimid period, eleventh–twelfth century.

Title-page: The prayer-hall of Qarawiyin Mosque, Fes, built during
the first half of the twelfth century.

This page: The Christians prepare for war: a detail from a thirteenth-century
fresco depicting the conquest of Majorca.

© 1980 Orbis Publishing Limited
First published in Great Britain by Orbis Publishing Limited, 1984

Reprinted 1985

Typeset in Great Britain by Vantage Typesetting, Southampton

Printed in Great Britain by
Purnell Book Production Limited
Member of the BPCC Group

ISBN 0 85613 279 9

CONTENTS

PROLOGUE

The upper chapel of the palace of the Kings of Majorca at Perpignan. The Kingdom of Majorca, ruled by a branch of the royal line of Aragon, was separated from the Kingdom of Aragon for about fifty years at the beginning of the fourteenth century, before it was re-absorbed into the parent state.

At Perpignan in the far south of France two chapels, one above the other, face the entrance to the courtyard of the palace of the Kings of Majorca. An echo lasting for at least twelve seconds gives the small dark chamber of the lower chapel the dimension of a cathedral. The resonance comes partly from two wide shallow alcoves like loudspeakers facing into the room from the corners on either side of the sanctuary. They catch the eye at once, for after centuries of neglect they are, apart from the ceiling, almost the only features to retain their fourteenth-century decoration. The heads of the alcoves are rounded, not in globular fashion like half domes, but conically like half-funnels sloping inwards to a vanishing point at the back of the recess. From that vanishing point stripes of colour spring out like the rays of the rising sun towards the low round arch above each alcove, seeming to cast a halo on the surface of the wall above. The halo, a curving band around the arch of each recess, forms part of a painted frieze running continuously round the room, lifting only to enclose the narrow doorway, and to outline the two startling fans of red, blue, green and gold in the far corners. The frieze itself is red, patterned in black or dark blue with a geometrical design of oblongs and lozenges like embroidery on canvas. The design is indeed abstract, in curious contrast to the figurative art which can still be seen in the elaborate foliage of the carving in the vault. Still more can the contrast be appreciated in the upper chapel, where the alcoves and the frieze recur, but the carving is of apostles and saints, and the long windows of stained glass recall the churches of northern Europe. The origin of the design is rather indicated by the long curling tendrils of gold which bind the elements of the pattern together in their flowing arabesques. It is the writing of another language, another world, turned by the ignorant into a meaningless combination of horizontal and vertical blocks. The language is Arabic, and the words, distorted out of all recognition apart from the general resemblance to the original script, most probably contained the crucial phrase: la ilah illa 'llah wa Muhammad rasul Allah – 'There is no god but God, and Muhammad is the Messenger of God.'

THE WAXING

The pillars of the prayer-hall of the Great Mosque of Cordova, begun in 785 by the Amir 'Abd al-Rahman I, and enlarged three times over the next two hundred years. Line upon line of columns, which in the earlier part of the hall were re-used from Roman and Visigothic buildings, run from north to south to the wall which contains the mihrab, the niche which indicates the direction of prayer. They support the rows of arches carrying the beams of the flat wooden ceiling and the gables of the roof. Since the columns were short, the height was obtained by constructing each row of arches in two tiers, one above the other. Their branches curve above the aisles that open endlessly between the trunks of this forest of stone.

Roderic, King of Spain, was doomed. When, according to the legend, he ascended the throne in the city of Toledo, he refused to follow the custom of his ancestors and affix one more lock to the door of the House of Wisdom. Instead he demanded that the door be opened, and to the horror of his people, entered. There he found the table of Solomon, son of David, gold and silver, studded with jewels. Upon the table was a casket, upon whose sides were horsemen armed with lances, bows and drawn swords, dressed in skins with turbans on their curly hair. Inside the casket was a parchment on which was written: 'When this House and this casket which have been so wisely locked shall be opened, then shall the nation shown upon the casket enter the Island of Andalus, and its kingdom shall be blotted out.' At these words, King Roderic wept for what he had done, but it was too late. The army of the Arabs was upon him. In the great battle, he saw the figures on the casket live before his eyes. Terror took him even as Tariq, the leader of the fearful host, cut him down.

The tale is prophetic, its conclusion foregone. For those who wrote it down, the Arab conquest was an accomplished fact. For them it was only right that the greatest event in history, long prepared by the will of God, should have been marked by such portents as the time drew near. In the year 711, when the invaders crossed the Straits of Gibraltar, they already ruled land stretching to the borders of India and Central Asia. Destroyers of the ancient Persian empire, conquerors of the lands of Syria and Egypt from the empire of Byzantium, God was clearly with them. The acquisition of Spain was yet further proof of His favour.

Fidelity was the explanation, for the conquerors as for their successors. The victors belonged to a religious community. Those who had been the first to join, almost a hundred years before the defeat of Roderic, had sworn to keep faith with God and man. They were the Arabs, who were known in consequence as the *mu'minun* or faithful, their leader as the Amir al-Mu'minin or Commander of the Faithful. Non-Arabs whom they admitted were required to submit to the God of the Arabs and to the Arabs themselves. That submission was called *islam*, and the *muslim*, the man who made it, became the personal client of the Arab who received it. Together, the Arabs and their clients formed an army.

When Egypt was conquered in 642, the Egyptians were too valuable as tax-paying subjects to be allowed to enlist in this way. The Arabs however were few in number, and needed recruits and allies for the conquest of North Africa. To the west of the Nile, in the Libyan desert and the Atlas mountains, were the Berbers. Almost literally they were barbarians, peoples who had lived on the fringe of the Greek and Roman world while continuing to speak their own language. That language, whose dialects were spoken as far away as the Atlantic, was a distant relative of the Arabs' own Semitic speech. The people themselves wandered in the desert with their flocks and herds, grew dates in their gardens in the oases, or lived in villages in the hills and valleys of the Atlas. They were clannish, governing themselves by family custom, and settling disputes by the feud. Wise, warlike and wealthy men would be respected and obeyed, but not always or as a matter of course.

The Arabs advanced by raiding. Prisoners were taken and enslaved, some to be sold, some to be inducted into the army as muslim clients. Thereafter, a regular supply of slaves and recruits was assured by treaties which exacted a tribute of men, women and children from the Libyan peoples. Around 670 the armies were ready to attack Carthage, the provincial capital of the Byzantines in North Africa, as part of a general assault upon Constantinople. The assault, ordered by the Commander of the Faithful at Damascus, was designed to wipe out the Greek empire, which, with its imperial city on the Bosphorus, was all that remained of Rome. For once the Arabs failed. Nevertheless they established a *qayrawan*, a 'caravan' or camp some eighty miles to the south of Carthage.

Situated at the foot of the hills which divide the dry lands of the south and east from the higher, more fertile country to the north and west, the qayrawan was on a natural frontier between the desert and the climate of the Mediterranean. It was laid out in a square, its sides facing north, south, east and west. In the middle was a structure, perhaps a fortified enclosure housing the commander, serving as a place of refuge, meeting, drill and worship, even as a market. Here the Arabs gathered with their Berbers, their women and children, so that the qayrawan turned into a city of the same name, Qayrawan, usually spelt Kairouan. Disciplined by mass praying and preaching, they went out to capture Carthage in the last years of the seventh century, destroying the ancient city and settling at Tunis a few miles away. With much greater difficulty they subdued the Berber tribes whose princes saw themselves as rightful heirs to the Christian emperors in this, the land of Africa.

Africa, pronounced by the Arabs Ifriqiya, stretched from Tripoli into eastern Algeria. When finally conquered, it became an Arab province. At Kairouan, the new capital, the central area was rebuilt specifically as a mosque, a place of worship, while the governor occupied a 'government house' opposite the south wall. The Latin-speaking Christian population became subjects like the Egyptians, obliged to pay all their old taxes with the addition of a poll-tax upon every adult male. The Berber peoples of the mountains and the deserts, on the other hand, made their submission to the Arabs and to Allah, the One God, providing the army with yet more recruits, and with allies to join them when they took the field. Berber chiefs became the personal clients of Arab leaders. In this way, when Musa ibn Nusayr became governor in 705, Ifriqiya became the base for the conquest of the whole of the *Maghrib*, 'the West'.

The armies advanced rapidly across the Algerian plateau to Tlemcen, then on to Tangier. From the port of Ceuta Tariq, the Berber client and general of Musa ibn Nusayr, crossed to the Rock which bears his name, Gibraltar, Jabal Tariq, 'Tariq's Mountain'. Before him lay the kingdom of the Visigoths, descendants of the Germanic barbarians who had overrun Europe in the fifth century. From Toledo the Visigoths ruled in Spain as a warrior aristocracy, based on the old Roman towns, but owning great estates in the countryside. As Christians, they were closely allied to the Church. In 711 their king, Roderic, marched south to meet

Elvira ware, from the district of Granada in the time of the Umayyad caliphate of the tenth century. The bottle, whose neck is missing, is decorated in green and manganese with the figures of four hares. The liveliness and humour of the animals, conventionally rendered within the limits of the geometric design, are one of the charms of the pottery of the period in North Africa as well as Spain.

Tariq's forces. He fell in battle near Cadiz, and Tariq went straight inland to secure the royal treasure at Toledo. Musa ibn Nusayr followed with his Arabs in 712. The Visigoths, who had remained aloof from their Spanish subjects, Christian and Jewish alike, vanished within a century into the ranks of the conquerors. Only a name like Ibn al-Qutiya, 'Son of the Goth-woman', served as a reminder.

Musa and Tariq returned to Damascus in 715 with fabulous booty, including the 'Table of Solomon' said to have stood in the House of Wisdom. It was a high point in the history of the Umayyads, the dynasty which held the office of Commander of the Faithful by hereditary right. King Roderic joined the emperors of Persia and Byzantium and the king of Abyssinia among the vanquished foes portrayed on the walls of the Syrian palace of Qusayr 'Amra. Spain, 'the Island of Andalus', was added to the immense realm ruled through a governor in Kairouan. Its capital was Cordova on the Guadalquivir, the *wadi al-kabir* or 'great river', where the Arabs occupied the castle with a space nearby for muster and worship. The invaders gathered tribute in cash and kind, while their leaders parcelled out the land.

No one was content. Musa and Tariq quarrelled. Musa's son was murdered after his marriage to Roderic's widow. At Kairouan the governor Yazid was assassinated by his Berber guard. These rivalries and jealousies were only suppressed by continuous conquest. Annual raids scoured the borders of the desert, sailed in pirate fleets to Sicily, Sardinia and the Balearic Islands, and crossed the Pyrenees to the Loire. As men flowed westwards out of Egypt to share in the plunder, slaves flowed back along the thread of a route from Cordova through Tangier, Tlemcen, Kairouan and Tripoli to the east. Allied Berbers joined in the forays against their unsubmitted neighbours, and moved in large numbers into Spain. There they revolted against the division of the land and the division of the booty, of which a fifth went to the treasury, and the remainder to the troops in very unequal portions, a horseman for example receiving three times as much as a foot soldier. In North Africa they rose in massive rebellion at the attempt to tax them like non-members of the community, having not only their young men taken for the army but their daughters for the harems of Damascus, and their ewes killed to obtain the soft and valuable skins from the unborn lambs.

The conquests came to a halt. Within the army, the Berber regiments resented the Arabs. The Arabs were divided into factions according to their tribal origins in North and South Arabia. Those of long standing in the west opposed the new men who came from the east with each successive governor. The governors themselves arrived with retinues of slaves and clients, guards and companions, whom they appointed over the heads of the powerful Arab nobles of the local province. As Arab horsemen were overwhelmed in Morocco by hordes of Berbers, Andalus cut itself off from the empire and turned to civil war.

The conflict spread throughout the empire. Not only the authority of the Commander of the Faithful was threatened. The very existence of the Umayyad dynasty was at stake. In North Africa, the Berbers claimed for themselves the right to choose the caliph or successor to the Prophet Muhammad as leader of the community. The caliphs they proclaimed one after the other at Tangier and Tunis were of obscure origin; they were overthrown by their own followers, or defeated by the Arab nobles, who seized Ifriqiya and kept it for themselves. From the other end of the empire, however, came the demand for a caliph from the actual family of the Prophet. In support of this demand, the Arabs and Persians of Khurasan in Central Asia united in a great uprising. Marching under their

Fatimid horseman, on a plate from the site of the Fatimid palace of Sabra outside Kairouan, tenth–eleventh century AD. The bold drawing of the face and the large eyes derives from the expressive art of Coptic Christian Egypt which developed from origins in the late Roman period to give this vigorous, if stylized, representation of a rider armed with a spear, dressed in a striped tunic, with a turban whose end is wound round and round the neck. In the absence of armour and other weapons, he may be a huntsman rather than a warrior.

black banners, they advanced upon Damascus. In 750 the Umayyads were overthrown and massacred. Their place was taken by a person who claimed descent from 'Abbas, the uncle of the Prophet. Fleeing from the slaughter, one of the few survivors of the fallen Umayyad dynasty, the prince 'Abd al-Rahman, arrived in Spain in 755.

Within a year he was accepted by the warring parties, and became the ruler of an independent state. Until his death in 788, he used the Berbers and the more recently arrived Syrians to repress the Arabs who had come with Musa ibn Nusayr and their allies from the old Visigothic nobility. The Syrians he overcame with a retinue which swelled into an army of guardsmen, some Berbers, some perhaps Negroes, but increasingly men from the north, from across the Pyrenees. These men, bought as slaves, trained as soldiers and then freed, were known as Slavs; they were 'dumb men' who spoke no Arabic and owed no loyalty except to the prince. The royal household, lodged in the fortified palace at Cordova, expanded into a government of chamberlains and viziers.

In North Africa, meanwhile, the new 'Abbasid dynasty failed to gain control of the Maghrib. Ifriqiya became independent under the Arab soldier Ibrahim ibn al-Aghlab. The Berbers to the south and west lapsed into autonomy, and in northern Morocco the city of Fes was founded by another refugee from Arabia.

The ruler's task was hard and bloody. 'Abd al-Rahman and his offspring inherited a country whose conquest was not complete. Away to the north, the kings of the Asturias and the Basques of Navarre had resisted incorporation into the Arab dominion. They were too primitive as yet to pose a real threat to the Arab hold upon al-Andalus, and refused to join with Charlemagne, the King of the Franks, in his attack upon the Arab outpost of Saragossa in 778. The Basques, indeed, captured his retreating baggage train in the pass of Roncesvalles, killing Roland, Duke of Brittany, the commander of the rearguard. Christianity was nevertheless beginning to strengthen the determination of the northern

Above the doorway of the Caliph Hakam II in the western wall of the Great Mosque of Cordova, the three-dimensional arcades of the interior have been compressed into a single row of interlocking arches carved in relief in the red and white stone. The horseshoe arch of the doorway itself, and the lobed or foliated arches which enclose the pierced stone lattices to either side, reproduce the forms of the mihrab and of the arches which surround it inside the prayer-hall. The motifs drawn from the space within the mosque for the ornamentation of the flat exterior were copied not only in Muslim Spain but Christian Europe.

Spaniards to fight the enemy in the south. From the upper valley of the Ebro, over the mountains and down the Duero to the Atlantic, the northern uplands were a vast frontier zone fought over by raiders and expeditions out for plunder. Watching over these borderlands, remote from the capital at Cordova, the cities of Merida, Toledo and Saragossa, enterprising and warlike, were a continual danger to the central government. In 797 Toledo rose against 'Abd al-Rahman's grandson. Its leading citizens were massacred by the new Amir, and their bodies thrown into a ditch. Royal uncles and cousins brought the peril home to Cordova itself. In 808 conspirators plotted in favour of a cousin of the prince. Seventy-two were killed and crucified along the street from the great Roman bridge over the river.

Monarchy of this kind was nevertheless the successful type of government to emerge from the Arab conquests. As it became established in the ninth century, the religion likewise assumed a definitive form. The mosques, the 'places of worship' in the middle of the garrison cities, were built and rebuilt in the course of the eighth century in increasing size and splendour. The north-south-east-west orientation was maintained. Thick walls, turrets or a high tower might still give the building the character of a fortress. A courtyard surrounded by a colonnade gave access to the prayer hall, in which row upon row of arches stretched away on either side of a central aisle. At the far end of the aisle, in the middle of the long south wall, was the arch of the *mihrab*, the semicircular recess which indicated the direction of prayer. In the dimness of the hall it was the one

The fluted dome above the mihrab of the Great Mosque of Cordova, built by the Caliph Hakam II in 965, is an ancient symbol of heaven. It is carried by a vault of interlacing arches, far heavier than the timber of the prayer-hall roof. To bear the weight, the arches on the lines of columns down below have been built across as well as down the aisles to form a box-like lattice whose intersections can be seen on the left-hand side of the picture, a rich delicate screen for the mihrab itself.

13

bright spot, lit by the windows in the dome overhead. By it stood the pulpit, from which the *imam* or leader of the congregation addressed the people in the great prayer at midday on Friday. It was an act of policy as well as piety on the part of the ruler to provide a suitable setting for that solemn moment when the sermon was preached in his presence and in his name as the true leader of the true people. The parade of loyalty was repeated in every prayer hall throughout the length and breadth of his dominions. So the Great Mosque of Cordova, begun by 'Abd al-Rahman I in 785, was enlarged by 'Abd al-Rahman II in 848; that of Kairouan was completely reconstructed in 836, and finished in 863. This growth kept pace with the growth of the community, as it turned from an army of occupation into a cross-section of the population.

The members of that community were the people of the Sunna or Custom of the Prophet, the rule by which they lived. Its framework was provided by the regular ritual of worship from the daily prayers to the annual fasts and pilgrimages; the call of the *muezzin* to the faithful to pray was a sign as characteristic as a Christian bell. Within that framework, the Custom was the Law by which the people strove to follow the example of Muhammad.

Originally the law of the community had been decided by the Commander of the Faithful upon his own authority. By the ninth century, however, it was firmly based on Scripture. It had become the Shari'a, the Law, a divinely perfect code of behaviour, revealed to man in the Koran, the word of God spoken to Muhammad, and in the sayings and doings of the Prophet recorded in the Traditions. Such a Law could

Leaf from a Koran of the ninth century from Iraq, the seat of the 'Abbasid caliphate, and the centre of the Islamic world of its time. The Kufic script, named after the city of Kufa on the Euphrates, was employed for the sacred text of the Book of God, and for inscriptions in stone, mosaic, tile and wood as far as Andalus. The influence of Iraq was not only religious, but extended to the courtly life of the Umayyads of Spain, who despite their hostility to the 'Abbasids, eagerly imitated the refinements of life in the palace cities of Baghdad and Samarra.

not be made or altered in any way by men, only learnt and obeyed. The interpretation of the Scriptures – to obtain a ruling upon any aspect of human life, worshipping, inheriting, possessing, paying taxes, buying and selling, fighting, stealing, killing – was a matter for qualified scholars or jurists. These handed down their wisdom from master to pupil, so that the authenticity of the faith from the time of the Prophet to the present day was guaranteed. To clarify their understanding, the jurists employed a classroom technique of question and answer. Sahnun, the great jurist of Kairouan, used the technique systematically in his *Mudawwana*. Framing his points in the form of questions put to a leading authority, he gave a complete exposition of the Law according to the Malikite school. This was the school which had originated with the jurists of Mecca and Medina, as distinct from those of Syria and Iraq, and became the principal school of Law in the west.

These jurists were not judges. The most they would do was to give an opinion on any question addressed to them, about what the Law should be in that particular case. Such an opinion was not a judgment which had to be carried out. The men of wisdom, who guarded the Law from corruption, stood in pious horror of its enforcement. Human decisions could never be perfect, and a binding judgment necessarily contained an element of error, however small. The man who pronounced it fell into sin. Enforcement of the Law was a matter for the *sultan*, the ruler or 'man of power', whose task it was to see that the world obeyed the divine command.

For this purpose, the sultan was assisted by the *qadi*, an official originally appointed to judge on behalf of the ruler in all matters within the community of the faithful. As the divine character of the Law became clearly established in the course of the eighth century, the prestige of the qadi increased, until he enjoyed an authority in his own right as the official representative of the divine commandment. The Qadi Ibn Ghanim refused to rise even in the presence of the ruler of Ifriqiya. Appointment to the post was nevertheless resisted by the jurists. When forced to accept the office, Sahnun declared: 'Today I am slaughtered without a knife.' From the monarch's point of view, the court of the qadi, with its rules of procedure and evidence, was slow and inefficient. Exercising his prerogative, the sultan would reserve to himself all criminal matters, complaints against injustice, and questions of taxation, which he would judge as he thought fit. The qadi, who judged in accordance with the Shari'a, came to be restricted to matters of ritual, decency, private property, marriage, inheritance and the like.

On the whole the jurists, the men of wisdom, collaborated with the men of power. Scholars might condemn; nevertheless, as they lectured the groups of disciples who sat around them in the colonnades of the great mosques, they insisted on the need to obey even the most unjust of rulers if protest failed to move him. In general the jurists were willing to use the Law to sanction the doings of the prince. However, the tradition of prayer and preaching which had turned the Arabs and Berbers into an army, and set off the great revolts which overthrew the caliphate of the Umayyads at Damascus, did not run out tamely in the prayer halls and courtyards of the great mosques with sermons from the pulpit, the lessons of the scholars and the judgments of the qadi. Inside but also outside the mosques, more popular preachers harangued their audience. Learned or unlearned, many were ascetics, men of ferocious holiness quick to rouse the mob for righteousness. The impious monarch who ignored the known custom in his desire for power risked a furious anger.

Riots for the faith provoked a massacre of the population of Cordova

La ilah illa 'llah: 'There is no god but God'; the inscription surrounds two seated figures in the Garden of Paradise. The weaving of silk was introduced into Spain from the Middle East in the ninth century by the Amir 'Abd al-Rahman II, together with the tiraz factories or palace workshops in which the cloth was made and fashioned into robes. Tiraz was the name of the cloth, but came to designate in particular the long bands of inscriptions which were often the only ornament. Cordova was the first centre of the industry in Spain, but was later eclipsed by Almeria. The value of the fabric, enhanced by the use of gold and silver thread, was matched by the splendour of the pictorial motifs, Egyptian and Persian in style, but far older in origin, going back to the art of ancient Mesopotamia, in which symmetrical figures confronted each other on either side of a tree or other upright.

This is a detail of a fragment from a large silk and gold hanging found in the tomb of Bishop Gurb (d. 1284), in the Cathedral of Barcelona.

by the Amir Hakam I, and the exile of many more. In the course of the ninth century, however, this dangerous zeal was diverted into holy war upon the foreign infidel. In 827 the men of Ifriqiya embarked upon the long conquest of Byzantine Sicily. Zeal itself was institutionalized. The coast of Ifriqiya had been defended by a kind of fortress called a *ribat*; garrisons of archers kept a sacred watch for the Byzantine fleet, their hours of vigilance measured by the hours of prayer. Such *murabitun* or men of the ribat were to be found upon the inland frontiers of Andalus, carrying on the holy war as a matter of routine. As the conquest of Sicily advanced, however, the ribats of Ifriqiya lost their military character. Their inhabitants became devotees who lived like soldiers but without a soldier's task. While ribat became synonymous with holy war, it acquired the second meaning of a life of more peaceful holiness.

The enthusiasts who rushed to Sicily for booty, land and trade were members of the Muslim community. By the ninth century, Islam with its

The Muslims besiege the Byzantine city of Messina in Sicily, which they captured in 842–3, although the Greeks held out at Taormina to the south for sixty more years. The 'Saracens' are seen here through Byzantine eyes in the illuminated Chronicle of the eleventh-century historian John Skylitzes. Their turban-like headdress is their distinguishing feature.

meaning of submission to God alone had become the proper name of the religion of Allah. Those who made the profession of faith were received into an army of the spirit rather than the flesh. They belonged to a House of Islam which stretched from the Atlantic to the borders of India and China, traversed from end to end by merchants and craftsmen, scholars and refugees, soldiers and statesmen. Many from east and west got no further than Kairouan. The great city with its mosque, its scholars and its princely court, feeding off a wide area in a barren spot on the arterial route from Andalus to the Indies, was the epitome of a civilization that extended across the known world. The energies which had created it, religious, military, political, commercial and colonial, ran on into Sicily to produce yet another Muslim nation in another land.

In North Africa the Muslim population was growing by natural increase, by the import of slaves from Europe and the Sudan, and by the drift of tribesmen into the new society. Growth was accelerated by the colonization of the Atlas and the desert, less spectacular than the conquest

of Sicily but equally effective. Beyond the borders of Ifriqiya, those
Berbers who had taken part in the great revolts in the middle of the
eighth century had formed themselves into a sect whose members spread
over a thousand miles from the Libyan Fezzan to the plateaux of Algeria.
In the oases and among the nomadic tribes of the Sahara they had
organized the desert trade to supply the markets of the Mediterranean
with negroes from the central Sudan and a trickle of gold from the banks
of the Niger. Pushing westwards along the southern flank of the Atlas,
they encountered the Idrisids of Fes crossing the mountains to lay hands
upon the silver and copper mines of southern Morocco. Beyond them all
on the Atlantic coast were murabitun, 'men of the ribat'. As these
murabitun spread northwards over the high passes onto the northern
slopes of the High Atlas they settled in the valleys as venerable saints.
Migrants, merchants, warriors and holy men, moving further and further
from the original centres of Islam in the Maghrib, introduced themselves
into the most remote reaches of an immense land.

*The ribat of Sousse. Built about 780 as a
fortress, mosque and place of refuge for the
Muslim community of the small port in case
of Byzantine attack from the sea, it acquired
its tower as a lookout-post in 821. The dome
over the mihrab of the little prayer-hall on
the first floor stands above the simple
entrance; the battlements, provided with
arrow-slits, are repeated on the inside edge of
the parapet overlooking the court, so that the
roof could be defended even if the door were
stormed.*

The southern flank of the High Atlas of
Morocco, rising from the edge of the desert to
Alpine scenery at the crest of the range at
10–12,000 ft. The high pastures are summer
grazing grounds for the flocks of Saharan
nomads as well as for the animals of the
mountain tribesmen who live in the more
fertile valleys on the northern slopes. Berbers,
these tribesmen were proud to claim that they
had been conquered and converted to Islam by
the legendary heroes of the Arab conquest in
the seventh century. In fact, it was only in
the ninth century that the Idrisids of Fes
crossed the eastern end of the range in search
of the silver and copper in the Saharan valley
of the Dra and the irrigable land of the Sous.
The western end of the range was reached
and crossed from south to north by nomadic
merchants and holy men wandering westwards
along the northern edge of the Sahara from
as far away as Ifriqiya. The merchants who
colonized Aghmat on the plain of the Oued
Tensift to the north of the mountains, and
the murabits or holy men who settled in the
valley of the Oued Nfiss below Tinmel,
drew the Berbers of the mountains into the
expanding society and economy of the new
civilization of Islam. The murabits
especially, who could arbitrate in tribal
quarrels in the name of God, or combine the
tribesmen into a new Islamic brotherhood,
worked upon the peoples of the High Atlas
to transform them into a major force in the
history of the Muslim West.

The Latin-speaking Christians of Ifriqiya, outnumbered by the Berbers who succumbed to Islam without a struggle to keep a faith of their own, had dwindled away by the twelfth century. In Spain, where Christians were in the majority, and the hillmen of the north defied the Arabs with the Cross, their numbers declined in much the same way. Spaniards called *Muwallads* or 'adopted children' followed the Visigothic nobility and became as Arabs, speaking the new language and adhering to the new religion. Others, who came to be called *Mozarabs* or 'would-be Arabs', accepted the language while remaining Christian. They did so because Arabic rapidly established itself as the language of administration and polite society; knowledge of Arabic gave the educated Christian the qualification for a career in the fashionable world of the ninth century. Christianity was useful to a government in need of servants outside Muslim politics, although it might eventually be abandoned by such servants as they identified themselves with Arab culture. In futile protest at such behaviour, the priest Eulogius incited his followers to martyrdom by cursing the Prophet; their execution at Cordova was the prelude to a persecution which induced a wave of conversions in the capital.

More important was the success of Islam among the illiterate peasants for whom, as for the Berbers, Arabic remained a foreign language. Arab rule meant freedom after the serfdom of Visigothic days. As the economy expanded and the population began to grow, Muslims came to settle in the countryside around the main towns. The marriage of Christian women to Muslim men, never the oth way about, may have contributed to a disproportionate increase in the Muslim population. Despite the decline of Christianity, however, the Spanish dialect of Latin maintained itself in speech even for the most highly cultured Arab, perhaps literally as a mother-tongue. It resisted eclipse by vernacular Arabic, just as Berber survived as a language in North Africa.

In Andalus the Arab aristocracy, turning away from Berber women to fair-haired slavegirls from the north, became physically European within a hundred years. The flux of race, religion, language and culture, however, was not easily controlled. In Ifriqiya the Aghlabid dynasty ruled uneasily over a riotous populace in the cities and warlords in the hills. Berber peoples like the Kutama of the mountains of eastern Algeria, who suffered the depredations of these warriors, were ready to respond to the prophet who damned the government at Kairouan as an abomination of the devil.

The prophet was the missionary Abu 'Abd Allah. In Syria and Iraq the 'Abbasids were threatened by the kind of revolution which had carried them to power in the previous century. The coming of the *Mahdi*, the Rightly-Guided One, was predicted for the year 903. Heir to 'Ali and Fatima, the daughter of the Prophet, he would restore God's justice to earth. Abu 'Abd Allah, sent to prepare the way for the hidden master of the world, came to Ifriqiya from the Middle East, and triumphed. In 909 his Kutama hordes drove the last of the Aghlabids from Kairouan. The Mahdi 'Ubayd Allah revealed himself as the first of the Fatimid dynasty. From Ifriqiya the Fatimids planned to conquer Egypt on the way to Baghdad and the fulfilment of their ambition. Meanwhile they sent their emissaries into Andalus.

By this time the power of Cordova was almost extinct. The central government was hated, despised and ignored. From Saragossa in the north-east to Seville in the south-west, Muwallads and Arabs had seized power in the major cities. Often they had closer connections with the Christian principalities to the north than they had with the Umayyad capital. Pastoral Berber tribesmen wandered in the Tagus valley, while

Ziyad ibn Aflah, son of a favourite of the great caliph 'Abd al-Rahman III, head of police, governor of Cordova and eventually vizier, had a round ivory casket carved for himself in the year 969–70. The figure which may be himself, was represented sitting in judgment, hunting with horse and falcon, and in this detail, travelling in state, cross-legged in the posture of a king.

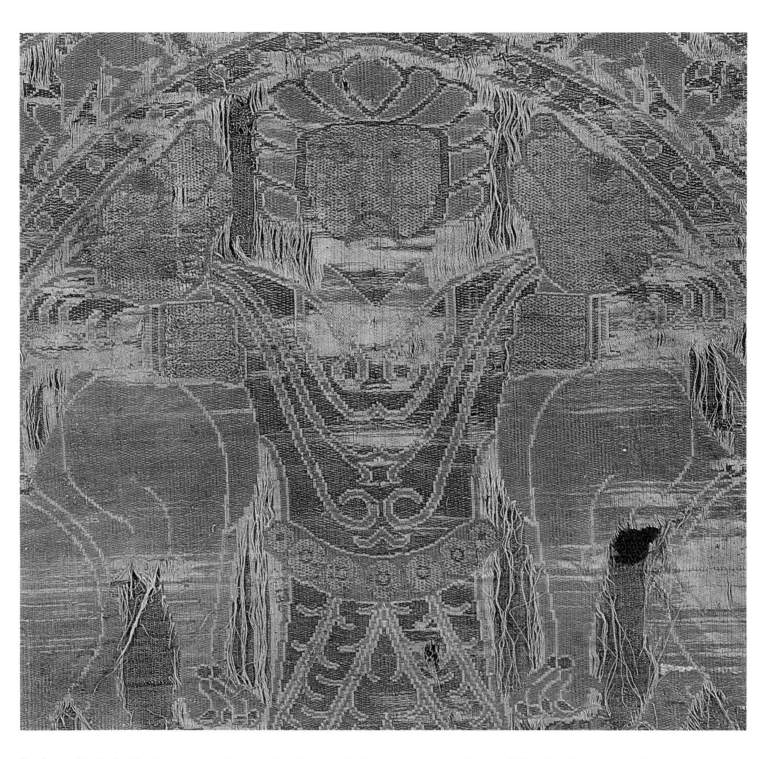

Berber chiefs held the mountains at the head of the river. From his stronghold of Bobastro in the mountains of Granada, the rebel Ibn Hafsun threatened Cordova itself.

Restoration began with the accession in 912 of 'Abd al-Rahman III, al-Nasir, 'the Victorious', at the age of twenty-three. Twenty years later, with Bobastro taken and Toledo captured after a long siege, the power of the dynasty had broadened outwards from Cordova to the frontier. The Umayyad amir once again became the Caliph, Commander of the Faithful, the undoubted successor of Muhammad as leader of the community in the direct line of his ancestors at Damascus. The title was assumed, after so many years, in reply to the claim of his enemy in Ifriqiya, the Mahdi 'Ubayd Allah, to be the true leader of the Muslim world. In the eyes of the people of the Sunna, the Fatimids were heretics, and the bitterness of religious hatred intensified the political rivalry. As

'The Lion Strangler'. The so-called 'Gilgamesh motif' of the royal hero whose strength is greater than the beasts, named after his prototype in ancient Mesopotamian legend, is reproduced in Persian style in the silk and gold of this fabric of the twelfth century in Muslim Spain. This is a detail of a textile found in the tomb of Bishop Bernard Calvo of Vich.

21

Above: Christian bell, perhaps as early as the ninth or tenth century, converted into a mosque lamp in the course of the eleventh century. Taken to Algiers, it was recaptured by the Spaniards in the sixteenth century.

Opposite: A doorway in the walls of the Alcazaba or citadel of Malaga, rebuilt in the eleventh century after the capture of the city by the ruler of Granada in the period following the end of the caliphate and the disintegration of the Umayyad dominion in Spain.

war broke out in North Africa, petty dynasties were swept away, and the Berber chiefs obliged to declare their loyalty to one side or the other.

Two great military empires, the Umayyad and the Fatimid, thus split the Muslim West. Their armies, in which regiments of well-trained infantry, Slavs, Berbers and Sudanese, gave stability to the volatile cavalry, had no equal on the battlefield. Only very occasionally did such an army blunder to defeat. Equipped with siege engines it could attack a fortress, or put to sea in a fleet of galleys. Its headquarters were in the palace, Umayyad or Fatimid, from which, in the conventional phrase of the chroniclers, 'no army set forth but it triumphed, and no banner flew except for victory'. At Mahdia, 'the city of the Mahdi' on the Tunisian coast, the palace was a mighty fortress; at al-Zahra', 'the Radiant' outside Cordova, it spread over many acres. Courts, gardens and pavilions housed the monarch, his family and his entourage, his guards and his ministers, thousands of occupants in a great royal city of residences, offices, barracks and quarters. At the centre the man himself moved like the sun. A strong personality was required to sustain the role in the midst of luxury, ambition and intrigue.

'Abd al-Rahman III, the great caliph, died in 961, his son Hakam II in 976. While Hakam collected books, the court plotted. When Hisham came to the throne at the age of eleven, he was quickly put aside by the chamberlain or chief minister Ibn Abi 'Amir. Under the title al-Mansur, 'the Conqueror', this man of humble origin ruled with ruthless efficiency in the name of the young caliph. Government was transferred to yet another palace city, al-Zahira, 'the Manifest', which the dictator built for himself upstream from Cordova. Annual campaigns which he led in person scoured the Christian north as far as the shrine of St James at Compostela. Christian captives brought back the doors and bells of the church to Cordova; the bells became lamps in the Great Mosque, which al-Mansur enlarged to its present enormous size. He was buried together with the dust of piety brushed from his armour over the years; as Almanzor he lived on in legend. At his death in 1002 the power of Andalus and its government had never been so great. Yet the system was fragile. Seven years later, lacking his father's ability, the second son of Almanzor was overthrown. As Cordovans, Slavs and Berbers in the government and in the army set up as many caliphs as they wished, the provincial cities revolted. In 1031 the Umayyad dynasty, its caliphate and its empire, came to an end.

Ifriqiya was overtaken by a similar fate. The Fatimids conquered Egypt, and left for Cairo in 972. Their lieutenants, the Berber princes of the Zirid dynasty, ruled at Kairouan in the face of religious opposition, declining prosperity and growing discontent. In 1048 the Zirid sultan Mu'izz repudiated his Fatimid overlord in Cairo in an effort to unite the country behind him. For a moment he appeared to succeed. Then an essential prop for his grand design collapsed. The beduin Arab tribes of the Banu Hilal, who had wandered westwards over the years from the Nile valley into the Libyan area, had been employed by the sultan to patrol the vital caravan route along the Libyan coast as far as Tripoli. Dissatisfied with this bare strip of country, they seem to have demanded the right to move further into Ifriqiya. Mu'izz went out to meet them as they advanced upon Kairouan. His army was ambushed and routed by the nomads, his support vanished, and his scheme fell apart. In 1057 he left Kairouan for Mahdia on the coast. Deserted by its ruler, the great city was abandoned by a host of its inhabitants. Only the jurists were left with their Great Mosque, the first in the Muslim West, to maintain the ancient capital as a centre of learning.

THE WANING

The Moors defend Majorca. The island was captured in 1229 by the Aragonese, and its conquest became a favourite subject of Catalan art. The frescoes—of which this is a detail—were painted about fifty years afterwards in the Palacio Berenguer de Aguilar at Barcelona by an unknown artist, thought to be himself a Moor. Moor, the name given to the Muslims of Andalus and North Africa by the Christians, derives from an ancient word for North Africans contained in Mauretania, the Roman name of northern Morocco. It acquired the sense of swarthy, even black or negro, apparent in Shakespeare's Othello, 'the Moor of Venice', so that eventually it became necessary to talk of 'white Moors'. The origin of the stereotype is presumably the number of negroes imported over the years as slaves from the western and central Sudan, and employed as servants and soldiers as well as concubines, so that it was possible to call the great Moroccan sultan Abu 'l-Hasan in the middle of the fourteenth century 'the Black'. But the image owes much to the identification of the followers of the rival faith with the black fiend, grotesque as the negro portrayed in the tower.

The Balearic islanders were noted for their use of the sling.

Zaynab the beautiful, so it was said, was the queen of Aghmat to the north of the High Atlas. Wooed by all, she refused, saying that only the man who ruled the whole of the Maghrib would marry her. Those she rejected hated her as a witch with second sight, to whom the genies from below the earth would speak. But when Abu Bakr, chief of the Sanhaja of the desert to the south of the mountains, presented himself, she agreed. Leading him blindfold underground, she showed him by the light of a candle a mighty hoard of treasure which God had given to him by her hand. Then in the same way she brought him out. On his return to the desert to fight his enemies, however, he gave Zaynab in marriage to his cousin Yusuf ibn Tashfin. From the city of Marrakesh which Abu Bakr had founded close to Aghmat, Yusuf conquered Morocco. When Abu Bakr came back from the south, he found the gates closed against him. He retired permanently into the Sahara, while Yusuf advanced into Spain. Thus the prophecy of the princess was fulfilled.

As with Tariq, so with Yusuf; legend has rewritten the beginning in the light of the end, employing the devices of the supernatural to tell a story worthy of its heroic theme. The man of destiny is none other than the saviour of Islam in the west, come to restore the faith by force of arms. The evils he fought were the evils of the world, an infidelity more shameful than the open disbelief of Christians and pagans. In the middle of the eleventh century Andalus was at the height of its prosperity and variety. The city states whose formation had been interrupted by the caliphate of 'Abd al-Rahman III had developed rapidly after the collapse of Almanzor's regime into fully independent principalities under the so-called Little Kings. This fragmentation solved the problem of government in Andalus, revealing the wealth and activity of the urban centres, enhancing their liveliness with each new court, each new patron. At Granada and Toledo the rulers were Berber, at Almeria Arab, and at Denia Slav. Racial animosity exacerbated the continual warfare between them, but remained confined within the limits of a common Arabic culture now reaching the height of its literary expression. Seville was the greatest, the richest and the most extravagant, whether it was the city of the father al-Mu'tadid, 'Divinely Helped', who filled a garden with the heads of his enemies and the earhole of each skull with a parchment to remind him of the name, or the city of the son al-Mu'tamid, 'Reliant on God', who turned a courtyard to a swamp of perfume for his queen I'timad, 'Reliance', and her ladies to paddle in barefoot like the country girls in the street.

To the north, however, the counts and kings from Barcelona to Galicia had recovered with astonishing ease from the drubbing of Almanzor, clear proof of the axiom of medieval warfare that victory in battle meant little unless followed by the occupation of enemy towns and fortresses. The military machine of the caliphate dismantled, the warbands of the Christians began to grow and join in a concerted push against a disjointed foe. As northern herdsmen drifted down into the no-man's-land between the Duero and the Tagus, first Navarre and then Castile exacted a tribute in gold from the Little Kings. The tribute which they shared out amongst themselves was spent in the first instance on land, horses, arms and armour, and secondly upon the pilgrimage route to Compostela.

St James, 'Santiago', was the patron saint of the struggle against Islam; his remote shrine in the far north-west had attracted pilgrims from all over western Europe since the discovery of his remains, miraculously brought from the Holy Land, in the ninth century. The route from the Pyrenees was provided with paths and bridges, and stopping-places after each day's journey. Many of these halts were monasteries founded by monks of the great French Cluniac order, who had been given the land on which to build. Others were towns colonized by French merchants invited to provision the pilgrim way. French involvement extended the organization as far back as Paris, Germany and Italy. Meanwhile the monks of Cluny, whose abbots were strong supporters of the Pope, helped to bind the provincial church of Spain to Rome, and to give the attack on Muslim territory the character of a crusade.

Mozarabs, the Arabized Christians of the south, found their situation alter as the interest of the Christian rulers in their fate estranged them from the Muslim populace. Muslim princes, on the other hand, willingly continued to employ men from the north as soldiers. Asturians, Basques and Catalans provided them with Christian mercenaries in place of the slaves imported for the purpose in the past. Northerners ready to sell their services in this way could expect a profitable career. The Castilian Rodrigo Diaz de Bivar fought for the rulers of Saragossa against Muslims and Christians alike, winning the title al-Sayyid al-Mubariz, 'Lord and Champion'. Speaking Arabic, living as an Arab, he moved easily between the two societies.

What removed his exploits from the politics of Muslim Spain, and transformed him, as El Cid Campeador, into the national hero of a Christian country, was the dimension of the conflict between the two religions after 1085. In that year Alfonso VI of Castile progressed from exacting tribute to actual conquest, capturing Toledo, the first great Muslim city ever to fall. From there the way to the Guadalquivir, the heart of Andalus, lay open. Mu'tamid of Seville appealed to the Moroccan ruler, Yusuf ibn Tashfin, for help. Yusuf inflicted a resounding defeat upon the invader near Badajoz in 1086, and in 1090 returned to sweep away Mu'tamid himself and all the Little Kings apart from the Banu Hud at Saragossa. The princes of Andalus ended their lives in captivity at Aghmat, 'Abd Allah of Granada writing his memoirs, Mu'tamid the poet lamenting his fate while his wife and daughters spun for a living.

The conqueror came from a people on the remote horizon of Islam. In the mountains of the High Atlas the murabitun or holy 'men of the ribat' had maintained their faith on the authority of the distant scholars of Kairouan. Echoing the determination of these jurists to rid Ifriqiya of the taint of heresy, they kept watch against still stranger doctrines rooted in the far west. In the 1040s a man called Ibn Yasin went southwards to the Veiled Men, the Berbers of the Sahara who muffled themselves to the

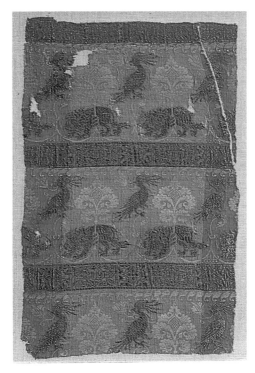

The Muslims of the West, who travelled the trade and pilgrimage routes which ran the length of the Islamic world from the Atlantic to China, would have recognized the Chinese influence at work in the cockatoos and lions of this piece of silk, which may be Central Asian or Persian in origin, or woven in Italy in the fourteenth century in imitation of the oriental fashion.

The tower of the Great Mosque of Kairouan, seen across the court from the entrance to the prayer-hall. The mosque, with its massive exterior wall of brick in the style of Iraq, and its tall fortified tower, was completed in the ninth century as the centrepiece of a great city. When the city was abandoned as the capital of Ifriqiya in the eleventh century, the mosque was left as a monument to past grandeur in a town of scholars and saints.

eyes. His very name marked him as a prophet. 'Son of Ya Sin': the Arabic letters Y and S which formed his patronymic were the title of a chapter of the Koran, and its opening verse:

> Ya Sin (Oh Man),
> By the Koran that prescribes and ordains,
> You are one of those who are sent
> On a straight road,
> A revelation of the Mighty, the Merciful,
> To warn a people whose fathers were not warned,
>   and hence are heedless and unaware . . .

A man of God, whose mission was so starkly given, he welded his followers into an army. Drilled by prayer, flogged for the slightest fault in their worship, they were called al-Murabitun, the Almoravids, because

Above: The gazelle or antelope, symbol of beauty and grace, metaphor for the beloved, exquisitely drawn upon a plate from the Fatimid period in Ifriqiya.

Below: The Oued Ziz flows southwards from the High Atlas to lose itself in the Sahara, bringing the route across the mountains from Fes down to the site of Sijilmasa in the oases of the Tafilelt, the starting-point of the journey across the Sahara to the Sudan.

like the men of the ribats of Ifriqiya they had bound themselves together in battle for the faith.

Warfare in the desert was transformed. The dashes of the horsemen centred round a mass of infantry, the front rank bearing long pikes to drive the enemy back, those at the rear armed with quivers of javelins. They stood when the standard was upright and sat down when it was lowered, motionless as mountains, never breaking in pursuit. Such a formation, made possible by the savage discipline of collective devotion, survived defeat in Mauritania and the death of Ibn Yasin in battle on the Atlantic coast of Morocco. Measured in its advance by the beating of innumerable drums, the army overran the Sahara and its fringes north and south. Crossing the High Atlas, it founded the city of Marrakesh. Under Yusuf ibn Tashfin the army took possession of the lands beyond the Atlas as far as Tlemcen. Giving thanks for its victory over Alfonso VI with a call to prayer from the pile of heads of the enemy slain, it reunited al-Andalus, incorporating the Green Island into a vast new empire on either side of the Straits. In battle against it the Cid won his renown, seizing Valencia and holding the town until his death in 1099, winning his last fight, so they said, when his corpse was sent out in armour on his horse against the foe. The Muslim city fell to the Almoravids only after his royal wife Jimena burned it behind her as she retired to Castile.

The Almoravids kept themselves apart from their new subjects. Garrisons in each major city were the extent of their presence. The strange veils of the men, the lack of veils and unusual freedom of the Saharan women, maintained the distance between them and those they ruled. Aloof, they ruled by the Law. Yusuf ibn Tashfin, taking the new title of Commander of the Muslims, relied on the approval of the jurists

for each major act. The jurists were paid, taken on campaign, introduced into the ruler's council, and appointed to bring the execution of justice into conformity with the Shari'a. In this way the elementary piety of Ibn Yasin became a policy of government.

The policy was in contrast to the normal practice whereby the sultan, the man of power, felt free to govern with only the most general blessing of the Law upon his administration. It was most popular in its attempt to reduce taxes to those prescribed by the Law, most divisive when intolerance drove Christians and Jews to emigrate northwards. Discontent among the native aristocrats of Muslim Spain, whom Yusuf ibn Tashfin had so contemptuously dismissed from power, increased under his son 'Ali. Brought up as a theologian rather than a warrior, 'Ali's harshness was more irritating than effective. But the regime was enormously rich; as Andalusian workmanship appeared on tombstones in the neighbourhood of Gao on the Niger, the gold of Ghana flowed northwards through Marrakesh. The Almoravid gold dinar swamped the silver dirham which was the standard currency of the Maghrib. Money in such quantities could buy not only luxury, which the Almoravids accepted as the reward of power and virtue, but also servants. For many years North Africa was policed by a strong force of Catalans. Whatever the shortcomings of the ruler, however serious the renewed incursions of the Christians into Andalus after the fall of Saragossa to the king of Aragon in 1118, the empire held firm until the death of 'Ali in 1143.

It collapsed in four years of bitter fighting against enemies on every side. The Almoravid example was infectious. The valleys of the mountains high above Marrakesh, from which Ibn Yasin had departed for the Sahara, now harboured another prophet. After years spent in the

Above: Gazelle in lustre on an opaque white glaze. Lustreware, like this Egyptian plate of the eleventh century, spread from the East in the Fatimid period to Ifriqiya and Andalus. Requiring three firings, for the base, the glaze and the golden paint, it was a major form of early Islamic pottery.

Muslim East, Ibn Tumart had returned to the Maghrib. Having denounced the immorality of Tunis, attacked the Saharan ladies as they rode barefaced through the capital of Morocco, and disputed the attributes of God with the scholars of the Almoravid court, he was forced to flee for his life to his birthplace in the hills. Among his own people, the Berbers of the High Atlas, his message became personal. Ibn Tumart revealed himself as the Mahdi, 'the Rightly-Guided', sent by God to restore the true faith on earth. The Masmuda tribes fell in behind him as al-Muwahhidun, the Almohads, those who proclaimed the Oneness of God.

From the impregnable site of Tinmel these Unitarians defied the Almoravids out on the plain below. For ten years after the death of Ibn Tumart his deputy 'Abd al-Mu'min, 'Servant of the Faithful One', waited; then about 1141 he led his troops away north-eastwards towards the Mediterranean, still keeping to the high ground, and in 1144–5 he began to threaten the Almoravid stronghold of Tlemcen. Though attacked by the new Almoravid amir Tashfin, the Almohads were victorious; Tashfin met his death as he fled, falling from his horse over a precipice at night. Leaving Tlemcen to be captured by a detachment of his army, 'Abd al-Mu'min advanced upon Fes, which fell in 1146 after a siege of nine months. Sending the brothers of Ibn Tumart on into Spain, the Almohad leader turned southward. Marrakesh held out for eleven months before it was taken and the Almoravids exterminated.

In Spain the Almoravid commander Ibn Ghaniya, attacked by Castile, was unable to contain the revolts which broke out on the death of Tashfin. As the Almohads entered Andalus, he fled to Majorca. Its military resistance at an end, the unpopular regime vanished. Nor was it immediately replaced. Christian Spain, consolidated into the kingdoms of Portugal, Castile and Aragon, now occupied more than half the peninsula. Having grown by conquest, these monarchies lived for more, seeking land to distribute to their nobles and new cities to tax. With the disappearance of the Almoravids they agreed among themselves upon the eventual division of the whole of Muslim Spain. Nevertheless, the various leaders of Andalus preferred alliance with these predatory neighbours to Moroccan rule. One, Ibn Mardanish in Murcia, took control of the eastern part of the country as a tributary of Castile and Aragon; the brothers of Ibn Tumart were forced to retire from Seville. 'Abd al-Mu'min, Commander of the Faithful, supreme ruler of the Muslim world in his capacity as caliph or successor, not of Muhammad but of the Mahdi, did not intervene. Instead, he turned to the conquest of Ifriqiya.

At the time when Yusuf ibn Tashfin conquered Morocco, and William of Normandy invaded England, other Normans carving a dukedom for themselves in southern Italy had begun to drive the Muslims from Sicily. By the time the Almoravids were overthrown, a Norman kingdom had arisen with its capital at Palermo, a state in which French, Italian, Latin, Greek and Arabic were equally familiar, churches and castles were built in the style of the mosques and palaces of North Africa, and a Muslim scholar might feel himself almost, if not quite, at home. Meanwhile, in the same adventurous spirit, the Normans took to the sea. The capture of Tripoli in 1146 was the first of several successes which gave King Roger II control of the Ifriqiyan coast as far as Sousse.

The flight of Hasan, the last feeble Zirid prince of Mahdia, to the court of the Almohad leader 'Abd al-Mu'min at Marrakesh, however, attracted a formidable opponent for the Normans. In two campaigns the Almohad host moved swiftly along a prepared route stocked with provisions and

A hawk holds the reins of a horse upon this Andalusian plate of the tenth century from Elvira. It is painted beneath the glaze in solutions of copper, sulphur and magnesium on a white ground.

30

lined with wells. The mountainous region of eastern Algeria was annexed; Tunis, which had become the greatest city of Ifriqiya, was captured. Keeping pace with the army as it moved eastwards, the Moroccan fleet sailing along the coast enabled 'Abd al-Mu'min to blockade the Normans in Mahdia by land and sea. Galleys sent from Sicily failed to break through. The garrison was starved into surrender as popular revolts expelled the Normans from the other towns along the coast. Inland, the Arab tribes were routed and promptly enlisted by 'Abd al-Mu'min for the war in Spain. As Ibn Mardanish, lord of Murcia, advanced upon Cordova, 'Abd al-Mu'min made ready his own forces for the conquest of Andalus in the fortress he had built for the purpose, Ribat al-Fath (the Ribat of Victory), from which Rabat has taken its name.

He died before the expedition could sail, in 1163. It was several years before the succession of his son Abu Ya'qub was assured, and his dynasty clearly recognized as the head of the Almohad movement. But Murcia was finally taken in 1172, and the whole of North Africa and Muslim

'One of the Gates of Paradise', where the faithful might win eternal life in battle against unbelief, the ribat of Monastir on the coast of Ifriqiya. It was drastically altered in the eleventh century and only the south side of the fortress, built in 796, was left standing with its little round tower in the midst of a large new castle with much higher battlements. The sanctity of the stronghold, however, was unaffected. While its walls offered protection against the Normans of Sicily, the ground outside became a cemetery. From 1057 to 1148, when Mahdia was the capital of the Zirids, the bodies of its rulers and its citizens were brought by sea for burial at Monastir in the shadow of the ribat.

31

Above: In this detail from a silk fabric of the twelfth or thirteenth century, perhaps from Almeria, the two figures who confront each other in the traditional manner within the roundel may be musicians, clutching and playing what could be tambourines. Between them hangs a lamp in the form of a vase, of a kind often made in painted glass. Textiles like this were given as tribute or received as presents, accumulated as capital or hoarded as treasure. They were sufficiently valuable to be used as money in large payments.

Opposite: The incomplete accomplishment. The topless tower of the unfinished Mosque of Hassan at Rabat, begun by the Almohad caliph Abu Yusuf Ya'qub al-Mansur in celebration of his great victory over the Christians of Spain at Alarcos in 1195, but abandoned at his death. In the architecture of this later period, the lobed arches surrounding the mihrab of the Great Mosque of Cordova have developed into panels of latticework which relieve the severity of these tall, straight minarets.

Spain united in a single empire. The brothers and the sons of the caliph were appointed to govern the major provinces, supported and sometimes replaced by the Almohad *shaykhs*. These, the leading tribesmen who had rallied the Masmuda around Ibn Tumart, now formed with their families the aristocracy of the movement which commanded the army and exercised a moral authority over the younger members of the royal family. From the children of these shaykhs was recruited a body of scholars brought up as gentlemen in the arts of war, but also as students of the doctrine of the Mahdi to preserve and defend it from corruption. Dressed in green tunics and white turbans, with woollen cloaks and leather sandals, they accompanied the sovereign on his journeys, and served as administrators appointed to the main towns. The army grew in size with the addition of professional troops to the ranks of the Almohad tribesmen who were called up for tours of duty in Marrakesh. Tribal levies were obtained from the warrior nomads of the Algerian plateaux and the plains of Ifriqiya, whose chiefs were commissioned to tax the country districts and keep them in order.

Andalus was heavily fortified. Alarmed by the might of the empire, the Christian kingdoms approved the foundation of three monastic orders of knights, Santiago, Alcantara and Calatrava, dedicated to the defence of the frontiers and modelled upon the Muslim concept of the ribat as an instrument of holy war. But the reconquest they feared never came. In 1184 the caliph Abu Ya'qub fell in battle against the Portuguese. His son and successor Abu Yusuf was promptly attacked from an unexpected quarter. The Almoravids who had taken refuge in the Balearic islands sailed for Ifriqiya. Sacking, besieging, capturing, ruling, 'Ali and his brother Yahya ibn Ghaniya gained control of the country. It required the caliph himself to drive them down into the Sahara. From Ifriqiya Abu Yusuf returned to face Castile. In 1195 he won the tremendous victory of Alarcos. Even as he did so, the Almoravids came back in the east.

The long march of the Almohad army to and fro across the Maghrib was the test as well as the proof of the empire's strength. Abu Yusuf, who took the title al-Mansur after the triumph of Alarcos, needed the impressive military demonstration at home as well as abroad. His father Abu Ya'qub, living in Seville, had been tolerant in matters of religion. The doctrinal difference between the Almohads, the followers of the Mahdi, who looked to the teachings of Ibn Tumart for guidance in the Law, and the Muslim population at large, who followed the traditional interpretation of the Shari'a by the jurists of the Malikite school, was not stressed. The attitude of the caliph was expressed in philosophical terms by his protégé, the philosopher Ibn Rushd or Averroes, who stood by the ancient opinion that there were two kinds of knowledge and belief, understanding for the élite and credulity for the masses. Abu Yusuf, however, living mainly at Marrakesh, close to the origins of the Almohads and to the aristocracy of shaykhs who were the leaders of their community, dismissed Ibn Rushd from court. More important, he prohibited the practice of the Malikite school, burning its books. Instead, the Law was to be applied in accordance with the teaching of Ibn Tumart, that jurists should go back behind the traditional interpretations of the Scriptures by the schools, and base their opinions directly upon the Koran and the Traditions.

This order to set aside the accumulated learning of the centuries, whose very continuity from master to pupil and book to book guaranteed its truth, was a denial of the deep conviction that the people of the Sunna or Custom of the Prophet had followed the inspired example of Muhammad through the years. So profound a reformation in the Islam of the

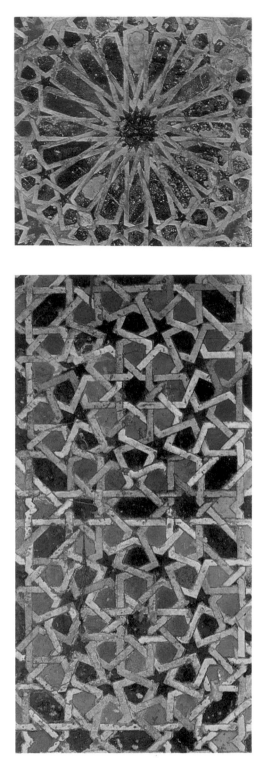

Tile mosaics from the destroyed Madrasa or college founded by the Ziyanid sultan Abu Tashfin at Tlemcen, 1318–37. Their intricate geometry extends outwards to infinity in patterns which took the craftsman a lifetime to learn to make from well over a hundred traditional shapes, each with its own name.

Maghrib, however, was not directed in the first instance at the Malikite majority, but at the Almohads themselves. By comparison with the Scriptures, the fundamental sources of the Law, not only the jurisprudence of the Malikite school was discounted. The interpretations offered by Ibn Tumart, the Mahdi or Rightly-Guided One himself, were deprived of authority. For the Almohads, it was an article of faith that the writings of Ibn Tumart, in which he expounded the meaning of the Koran and the Traditions, were themselves a form of Scripture which contained God's last word on the subject of His revelation. For the shaykhs, the military and religious aristocracy of the movement, the supreme authority of the Mahdi and his works was a defence against the inordinate power of the caliphs, the descendants of 'Abd al-Mu'min who ruled the empire. As guardians of the Mahdi's doctrine, they threatened to submit the monarch to their tutelage.

Abu Yusuf al-Mansur died in 1199 with his final monument, the Mosque of Hassan at Rabat, still unfinished. It was never completed. The doctrinal controversy rested, but under the new caliph al-Nasir, 'the Victorious', events propelled the empire decisively towards a solution. Their rhythm was that of the war on two fronts, from which al-Nasir tried to break free. In 1203 his fleet at last conquered the Almoravid islands of Majorca and Minorca. In 1205–07 he reconquered Tunis and its territory from the Almoravid Yahya ibn Ghaniya. The government of Ifriqiya was bestowed upon the greatest Almohad shaykh, Abu Muhammad al-Hafsi, who was given plenipotentiary authority to rule as a viceroy independently of Marrakesh. Relieved of responsibility for the province by this energetic and capable lieutenant, the caliph turned to meet the coalition building up against him in Spain. A Crusade was in the making, preached by the Pope, bringing knights from France, uniting the forces of Portugal, Castile and Aragon for a crushing blow. In 1212 the Almohad army, treacherously deserted, so they said, by the men of Andalus, was annihilated in the appalling battle of Las Navas de Tolosa. Only pestilence prevented the Christian advance. Al-Nasir retired to Marrakesh to abdicate and die.

The crisis came in 1227, when the caliph al-'Adil was murdered by drowning in a pool of the palace. At Marrakesh, the Almohad shaykhs seized the opportunity to proclaim their own candidate from the royal family. Their right to do so, however, was challenged by the dead man's brother, al-Ma'mun, the governor of Andalus. To deprive the shaykhs of any authority whatsoever, al-Ma'mun went far beyond his ancestor Abu Yusuf, the victor of Alarcos, in repudiating the Mahdi Ibn Tumart entirely. Where Abu Yusuf had maintained that the Rightly-Guided One's injunction to return to the Scriptures took precedence over his interpretations of the Koran and the Traditions, al-Ma'mun denied any validity at all to the Mahdi and his message. Instead he upheld the traditional doctrine of the Malikite school. Equipped by King Ferdinand III with a troop of Castilian knights, he crossed into Africa to capture Marrakesh and massacre the shaykhs. His hold on Morocco was maintained by his son, but his action was the signal for a rapid, drastic alteration of the scene throughout the Muslim West.

Deserted in this way by the descendant of 'Abd al-Mu'min, the Almohads found a new leader in Abu Zakariya', who succeeded his father Abu Muhammad al-Hafsi as viceroy of Ifriqiya. At Tlemcen the Berber prince Yaghmurasin changed from the loyal ally of the old caliphs into an independent ruler. In Spain Ibn Hud, descendant of the rulers of Saragossa, became master of the whole of Andalus outside Seville. However, when he refused to cede Cordova to his overlord, the King of

Castile, Ferdinand seized the city in 1236. This first major breach of the
Muslim frontier since the fall of Toledo and Saragossa over a hundred
years earlier was ruthlessly exploited. Aragon captured Valencia and
Portugal overran the Algarve. Ferdinand found a second Muslim ally in
Ibn al-Ahmar, an Andalusian of Arab lineage, who in 1246 ceded Jaen in
return for recognition as ruler of Granada. In 1248 with the help of
Granada the King of Castile took Seville.

For at least twenty years, during which time Murcia came into the
hands of Castile and only the mountains of Granada were left under
Muslim rule, the Christian kings remained at war with their new subjects,
expelling them from the cities to reward their soldiers with houses, and
driving them to revolt in the countryside as the farms were given to
Christian landlords; the lands which fell to Castile became huge ranches
owned by the nobility, on which sheep and cattle took the place of
agriculture. Only around Valencia did the Muslim population and its
economy manage with difficulty to survive. Refugees fled to North
Africa or crowded into the kingdom of Granada, where, in contrast, the
valleys and hillsides were cultivated with greater and greater intensity,
and a fierce Islamic patriotism existed alongside the careful diplomacy of
Ibn al-Ahmar and his descendants, the princes of the Nasrid dynasty.

The loss of al-Andalus, of its heartland in the valley of the Guadalquivir, was permanent. Seville, the greatest of its cities, became the capital to which the kings of Castile transferred their residence. There they lived like Arab monarchs in the civilized comfort of the south provided for them by the Muslim population which remained, known as Mudejar from the Arabic *mudajjan*, meaning 'tamed'. Muslim architects taught Christians to build in the Mudejar style. It was a curious situation in which the son of Ferdinand the Conqueror gained his title Alfonso the Wise from his patronage of Arab learning, while his regime dismantled the society of which that learning formed part.

As the Christian kingdoms digested their prey, they entered into relations with the new rulers of North Africa as well as Granada. At Tunis the Hafsids claimed sovereignty over the whole of the Muslim West. This overlordship, however, was nominal; the ideal of a great Islamic empire in the west retained its power over the mind, but in practice the appearance of separate states in each region put an end to the possibility of unity. Diplomatically, the states of the Iberian peninsula and North Africa, Muslim and Christian, formed a community in which attempts at aggrandizement were met by combinations of jealous neighbours.

The attack upon Tunis of King Louis of France with an army of Crusaders in 1270 ended as quickly as it began when the old king died of pestilence during the siege. Towards the end of the century Aragon posed a greater threat as it endeavoured to create an overseas empire out of Majorca and Minorca, Sardinia, Sicily and the coastal islands of Ifriqiya. Piracy and conquest, however, tinged with religious zeal, were

The Alcazar of Seville, rebuilt with Granadan assistance for Pedro the Cruel and the Just, King of Castile in the middle of the fourteenth century. Built around the courts which are the central features of its composition, the palace was the setting for the king's legendary adventures on nocturnal expeditions into the streets of the city. Dethroned, Pedro was briefly restored to his throne by Edward, the Black Prince, who invaded Spain in 1367.

subordinate to the commercial needs of Barcelona, the kingdom's great port. Its Catalan merchants traded with Tunis, which supplied the wool, wax and leather of North Africa, and passed on spices from the Middle East. The kings of Aragon, therefore, were normally content with an annual subsidy from the Hafsids, and a privileged position for their subjects in the ports of Ifriqiya. Equally favourable arrangements were made with the Ziyanids, the dynasty founded by Yaghmurasin, to obtain the gold coming through Tlemcen from the western Sudan. In 1291 Aragon secured from Castile the recognition of this special interest in the central and eastern Maghrib, in return for recognition of Castilian interest in Morocco.

Morocco, however, had re-emerged as a formidable power. Isolated in Marrakesh, the last descendants of 'Abd al-Mu'min were overthrown in 1269 by the Banu Marin, Berber tribesmen from the edge of the Sahara who had seized Fes, and in twenty-five years of fighting rebuilt a Moroccan state under their rule. Without either prophet or Mahdi to inspire them, the Marinids followed the example of Yusuf ibn Tashfin and 'Abd al-Mu'min. In 1275 they invaded Spain, defeating Castile, and taking sides in the quarrels of the Christian kingdom. At the end of the century they besieged Tlemcen for no less than eight years. With the accession of the great sultan Abu 'l-Hasan in 1331, Tlemcen was finally captured. In 1340, in battle on the Salado river against the combined forces of Portugal, Castile and Aragon, however, the Moroccan army was crushed by the massed weight of knights in plate armour. Four years later, after the defeat of the Moroccan fleet, the port of Algeciras was surrendered, and the long history of Moroccan invasions of the peninsula came to an end. Abu 'l-Hasan turned instead to the conquest of Ifriqiya. Tunis was occupied in 1347, but the sultan was overthrown by the rebellion of his son Abu 'Inan in Morocco, and died a fugitive in the snows of the High Atlas. Abu 'Inan recovered all that his father had lost in the eastern Maghrib, but the empire collapsed when in 1358 he fell ill, to be suffocated on his deathbed by the vizier anxious to place his own candidate on the throne. With him died the greatness of Morocco.

Granada under the Nasrid dynasty survived. The second half of the fourteenth century, when the whole of North Africa squabbled in the wake of the Marinid adventure, was a time of power and prosperity for the Spanish state. Granadan produce and manufactures, exported through Malaga and Almeria, earned the Sudanese gold with which its rulers bought their immunity from Christian attack. His borders secure, the sultan Muhammad al-Ghani, 'the Beautiful', was free to extend his influence across the Straits, promoting rival candidates for the Moroccan throne. His wealth allowed the completion of the Alhambra, the palace fortress overlooking a city which had grown into one of the richest in the peninsula.

But the world was changing. In the fifteenth century Portugal became militarily and politically powerful. As the Marinid kingdom shrank to little more than the region around Fes, the Portuguese captured first Ceuta, then Tangier and a string of ports down the Atlantic coast of Morocco. In 1479 Castile and Aragon were united in the persons of Queen Isabella and King Ferdinand. The union of the crowns was to be symbolized and strengthened by the purification of the faith, the elimination of the last Muslim state in Spain. Ten years of savage, stubborn war, in which one by one the fortresses of Granada were battered down or starved out, ended in January 1492, the year of Columbus, when the Catholic monarchs entered the Alhambra, and Abu 'Abd Allah, Boabdil, the last of the Nasrids, rode out into exile.

The Alhambra Vase, a superb example of the craftsmanship of the kingdom of Granada, gives its name to a whole class of such vases made at Malaga in the fourteenth century. Unglazed vases of this shape, with the two wing-like handles, were used for storing water, but these magnificent pieces of lustreware, standing over four feet tall, were never meant for anything except ornament. They carry multiple inscriptions, in at least one case an entire poem in gold, wishing the owner all honour, prosperity and good fortune.

THE FRAMEWORK OF SOCIETY

'When the Commander of the Muslims resolved to build a city for his kingdom and his government, to house himself and his court and his retinue, he rode out on Sunday the third of Shawwal in the year of the Hijra six hundred and seventy-four with the architects and builders and master craftsmen to choose the site on the river of Fes. The moment to commence digging was calculated by the learned mathematicians Abu 'l-Rabi' Sulayman al-Ghayyash and Abu 'Abd Allah Muhammad ibn al-Habbak, so that the foundation took place beneath auspicious stars, at a fortunate time, in blessing and favour which boded well for the long life of the city, the extent of its prosperity, and the continuance of its treasures and its revenues. When the walls of this fortunate city of New Fes were complete, the Commander of the Muslims Abu Yusuf ordered the building of the great mosque for the Friday prayer. The work was undertaken by Abu 'Abd Allah ibn 'Abd al-Karim al-Jududi and Abu 'Ali ibn al-Azraq the governor of Meknes, the cost being met out of the income from the olive oil-press at Meknes. Besides the master builders, only Christian captives from Spain were used for its construction. In the year six hundred and seventy-seven the great mosque was finished and inaugurated for prayer, and the construction of the present pulpit was begun by the master of inlay al-Gharnati, 'the Granadan'. Exactly a year later the pulpit was finished and employed for the address. In the year six hundred and seventy-nine the great chandelier was hung, weighing seven qintars and fifteen ratls (about 400 kilograms or 900 pounds), with no less than a hundred and eighty-seven glass lamps. It was made by the master al-Hijazi, 'from the Hijaz in Arabia', and paid for by the poll-tax on the Jews. In the same year the special enclosure to conceal the monarch from the public was erected in the mosque. At the same time the souks or market streets were built from the Gate of the Bridge to the Gate of the Sanhaja Springs. A great hammam or public bathhouse was installed, and the Commander of the Muslims, God have mercy on him, commanded all his ministers and governors to build each one of them a house within the walls. And this they did.'[1]

A royal city such as this one (built by the Marinids at the beginning of their rule in Morocco), was both the instrument and the symbol of government. Government was monarchical, and the city which was built to house the prince was a monument to his glory. That glory was

Sousse. The ribat in the foreground is enclosed by the walls built in 859, which reduced the little fortress to a hermitage for the devout ascetics of the garrison. Running up to the tower of the qasba on the hill, the walls were required to protect the much larger town which grew up after the invasion of Sicily in 827.

39

all the brighter for its subservience to God, the building of whose place of worship is the most carefully described. The means were required to match the ends. So the chronicler is careful to state that only Christian captives were employed as labourers, and that the poll-tax of the Jews was requisitioned to pay for the chandelier. Particular revenues were allocated to particular tasks as the income of the government was devoted to the noble enterprise, and contributions were requested from its servants and its subjects. Especially important were the master builders and the master craftsmen who were employed for the purpose, and whose names were so scrupulously recorded. Highly-paid experts, they moved from court to court and from patron to patron. By the year 1276, when the construction of New Fes began, their skills were fully equal to the task.

Massiveness and delicacy, running together in the architecture of the Muslim West, combined in the second half of the thirteenth century in a style which originated in al-Andalus, but extended eastwards as far as

Tunis. Great walls, towers and gateways, made necessary by war, were rendered elegant by their proportions, by the pointed, round and horseshoe arches of their entrances and windows, and by the panels of inscription and carved latticework upon the flat surfaces. The palaces and the places of worship which they contained were of a lightness weighted down by ornament. Plasterwork hung in stalactites from the domes and ceilings above the slender pillars, below the overhanging eaves of the green-tiled roofs. Deeply incised, the thick crust coated the walls in endless ramifications of leaves and letters. Carved woodwork, coloured tiles and sculptured marble spread out below. Arcades gave admission to the silent spaces of the mosque; they opened out of sumptuous interiors on to courts and gardens overlooked by galleries and balconies. Within its battlements the royal city, the place of power, was indeed a place of happiness, beauty and delight. Like the globe of an artichoke, the armoured casing protected a delicious heart.

Certainly it was a place of affluence, of wealth and luxury maintained by armies of domestics. However, with such a gigantic household, to which the principal servants of the sultan belonged, and to which they added their own princely families and followings, the enemy might well be within. The fortune of New Fes, unclouded by death, contrasts with the misfortune of its sister city, al-Mansura, 'the Victorious', built some twenty-five years later by the next Marinid monarch in order to blockade the town of Tlemcen. A long wall and ditch were thrown around the enemy capital to seal it from the world. Mansura grew from the tented camp of the besiegers. The new city had its own wall surrounding the

Above: The Aghlabid reservoirs at Kairouan were built in the ninth century to augment the city's water supply. The one on the left collected floodwater, allowing mud to settle before the water entered the larger tank. There it was mixed with water brought by an aqueduct from the hills, and fed into the tank through a cistern.

palace and the mosque, which was built over a great tank or reservoir filled by canals and aqueducts from the mountains. Three golden 'apples' or balls were placed one above the other on top of the minaret at a cost of 700 dinars. The finest houses, the most pleasant gardens were laid out; baths, inns and a hospital were provided. From all directions the merchants brought their goods to the flourishing markets. But when the sultan Abu Ya'qub suspected one of the ladies of his harem and arrested the chief eunuch as an accomplice, the others who served in the women's quarters took fright and conspired. Requesting entrance and receiving permission, the eunuch Sa'ada, a man with a woman's name, found his master lying on his bed while the henna with which he was elaborately painted slowly dried. The assassin stabbed the sultan in the stomach and fled. He was caught and executed, but Abu Ya'qub was dead, Al-Mansura was abandoned, the siege of Tlemcen was raised, and the entire city destroyed by the enemy as they broke out of their beleaguered town for the first time in eight years.

Two months later news of the murder reached an eminent gentleman seven hundred miles away at Ghoumrassen in the hilly country of southern Tunisia. Travelling in the company of a prince of the Hafsid dynasty at Tunis, the scholarly al-Tijani was encamped on the floor of a desolate valley to escape from pestilence in the city of Gabes while awaiting the arrival of a caravan bearing gifts from the sultan of Morocco to the sultan of Egypt. That caravan would take the party on to Cairo, from where al-Tijani and his royal patron would make the pilgrimage to Mecca and Medina, the Holy Places of Islam. With Abu Ya'qub dead, the Moroccan caravan was indefinitely delayed, and the prince and his entourage remained for a further two months in contemplation of the surrounding cliffs.

These cliffs were natural fortresses, inhabited by Berbers who made their homes in the numerous caves. Their small terraced fields and gardens were at the bottom, irrigated by channels from the streams which flowed after rain, the only pleasant sight in a barren land. The Berbers were effectively self-governing, either by the simple expedient of the feud in which groups of kinsmen took revenge upon each other for some original offence, or with the help of a council of elders who settled such feuds with a decision about the compensation due to the injured parties, and imposed strict rules of conduct on pain of expulsion from the community. In the same way they were at war with neighbouring Berber villages, although they might put aside their enmity on the neutral ground of some common market place. They were equally hostile to the nomadic Arab tribes who wandered up the valleys from the plain in search of pasture. The chiefs of these tribes represented the authority of the sultan at Tunis, who had granted them the territory as a kind of fief. The exercise of this authority took the form of Arab raids, causing the Berbers to withdraw to the security of their cliffs. At Ghoumrassen, however, a state of truce prevailed between the two peoples. One of the villagers, an educated man, acted as secretary to the Arab chief who claimed to rule this particular district. Because of this, the relationship between the two peoples was good, and the chief had dared to invite the royal party to stay as his guests so far from civilization. The place was completely safe, and no-one had anything stolen.

A garden in the barren hills of the Sahara, where beneath the burning sun, springs from underground run in channels among the date palms, 'head in fire and foot in water', which provide the shade for other fruits and vegetables on the ground below.

The independence of Ghoumrassen was nevertheless precarious. When the prince and his following at last moved on towards Tripoli, passing from the territory of one Arab chief to that of another, they skirted various Berber settlements along the coast which were said to be in a state of rebellion. They were fighting against the Arab domination of this section of the long caravan route to the east. At Zanzur they had failed.

The Berbers of Zanzur, living among their groves of date palms and olives, were divided into quarrelling factions, the largest clan being opposed by an alliance of smaller families. Each group was nevertheless subject to the Arab chief Salim or to one of his brothers and sons, who protected its members and taxed them by the trees planted and the area sown. The Arabs were in fact the landlords, the Berbers tenants who worked for them in good faith, and in return kept a portion of what they produced for themselves. Zanzur was the estate of an Arab lord, bestowed upon him by a charter of the sultan in recognition of his military prowess. Salim and his family were noblemen whose prestige as warriors had raised them politically, socially and economically far above their fellow tribesmen, whose camels fouled the waterholes along the way.

Estates of this kind were common, although not everywhere was the landlord quite so clearly the ruler and the tenants his subjects.

Above: 'Turning like a heaven without a star'; the noria or water-wheel, introduced by the Arabs from the Middle East, and one of the principal instruments of their agriculture.

Left: Irrigation in Morocco. 'Bringing to life the dead land' was an expression applied to any form of cultivation of the waste; when the ground was continually watered, the image was of Paradise.

Right: The harvest of corn and grapes, the threshing of the grain by horses and the pressing of the wine, from the Beatus of King Ferdinand I and King Sancho, 1047. 'Beatus' is the generic name given to the many copies of the Commentary on the Apocalypse written about 786 by Beatus, Abbot of Liebana, made by the Mozarabs, the Arabized Christians. Their art illuminates the dominant culture of Islam from a fresh point of view, in a style which combines elements from the manuscript painting of France and Britain with Islamic, Coptic and Byzantine influence.

Sharecropping was normal. Tenancies were least secure and least favourable on land where grain was grown without irrigation; the unwritten contract might be simply seasonal, and leave the farmer with only a fifth of the crop. Tenancies were more durable and more equitable on land planted with trees, which took time to bear fruit, and (which was often the same thing) on irrigated land, which was enormously valuable. This complicated parcelling-out was matched by the variety of ownership, from land collectively occupied in accordance with recognized custom by some tribal community to freehold property allocated to individuals in accordance with the Law. While in remote country districts the memory of these matters was fixed in the mind, nearer to the cities and the centres of government their intricacies were recorded in deeds of gift, sale and inheritance, the subject of endless litigation.

The range of agriculture was very wide. Grain was essential, cultivated with the light ploughs inherited from the Roman world. Trees, however, multiplied with species introduced from the east; an astonishing list of fruit-bearers from the emon and the Seville orange to peaches, pomegranates, bananas and figs were grown. Extravagantly, so the legend says, Mu'tamid of Seville covered the hills with almonds to please his queen with the effect of snow. New vegetables such as aubergines and asparagus were established along with important crops like rice, cotton and sugar-cane. Many clearly needed water, and irrigation developed with the aid of the *noria* or water-wheel, which scooped bucket after bucket into a basin which fed the channels. The regulations required to distribute the water from a single source to all the plots of all the proprietors, so that each had water running for the same length of time each day, survived into the Christian period along the Mediterranean coast of Spain. Laws governing the supply show traces of their origin in Syria and the Yemen.

Pastoralism was a way of life for the wilder peoples of the mountains, deserts and plateaux. Nevertheless it made an indispensable contribution to the economy. Meat was an important food; the sheep had a religious significance as the animal sacrificed by Abraham instead of his son. Butchers performed a religious duty when they cut the throat of an animal as prescribed by the Law. The skins and the wool went for leather and cloth. Even the most remote regions felt the pull of the market.

The market centred on the city, which lived off the countryside just as the countryside depended on the town. In the densely cultivated areas around the major urban centres the townsfolk, rich and poor, had their villas and summer-houses. The city itself, however, was quite distinct. When al-Tijani at last arrived at Tripoli, his eyes were dazzled by its whiteness under the sun. The governor vacated the citadel, and the royal entourage took up a residence which lasted no less than eighteen months, until the Moroccan caravan eventually arrived and the prince could proceed to Cairo in a manner befitting his rank. His scholarly companion spent his time writing verses to his friends, while making himself familiar with the place, its history and its antiquities.

The citadel normally occupied by the governor was large, dilapidated, and partly ruined. Much of it had been sold to people who had taken the stones and used them to put up their own houses. In the same way, the spacious gardens laid out below the citadel for the enjoyment of former rulers had been neglected by a new proprietor who had constructed a large residence on the site. Given this very characteristic kind of encroachment on the official spaces of the city, it was surprising that al-Tijani found the main streets remarkably straight, criss-crossing like the lines on a chess-board. Over the years the grid pattern which the Arabs had inherited from the Roman world had been transformed by a preference for houses facing inwards onto a court, built side by side and back to back with only the narrowest of façades above the single doorway. Main thoroughfares had become narrow and winding, while the side streets had become cul-de-sacs, little alleys branching to serve a cluster of houses through a single entrance off the public way. The compartments formed in this manner grew more pronounced with the habit of closing the entrances to the side streets with doors which could be locked and barred at night.

In the city of Old Fes the result has been compared to a lung that breathes in and out as the inhabitants flow into the public passages and places, and retire to their own particular enclaves. In Spain there is little left of such a structure. Only the Juderia or Jewish area near the Great Mosque of Cordova is a reminder that the compartments composed the quarters, and that the quarters were the units of community and government. This was true not only for the religious minorities, the Jews and the Christians, living according to their own law under their own authorities, who were responsible for their taxes and their good behaviour. Muslim quarters likewise developed their distinctive populations, perhaps by the immigration of a particular people from a particular place, perhaps by long residence. Old Fes was divided by the river into the Andalusian Bank, named after the refugees from Cordova in 814, and the Kairouanian Bank, after those who fled from Ifriqiya in the rising of 825. The distinction continued to be important, despite the proliferation of smaller districts and their quarters. Some of these quarters were rich, where the houses were large and occupied by one family. Others were poor, where the houses, still built to the same plan, were tenements with many occupants. Each had its headman appointed from the inhabitants.

Rich or poor, the quarters were distinguishable from the suburbs, amorphous settlements on the outskirts. At Cordova the very wealthy built their residences out towards the palace of al-Zahra'. Elsewhere the suburb might be a quarter of the city in the process of formation, or a place for casual workers and seasonal migrants. The town walls would normally make the distinction clear. As the art of fortification progressed, the walls became more substantial, less easy to alter. At Tripoli the people were engaged upon the digging of a great ditch around the walls to meet up with the sea at each end, but found that it filled with sand as soon as excavated. The expense of such works was considerable, and might be met from the revenues of particular fields and gardens, of a bathhouse or a tannery, just as the mosque of New Fes was built with money from the oil press at Meknes. Endowments of this kind were the normal way of providing for the maintenance of a mosque, for example, or a school or hospital. The charitable gifts which these institutions received in perpetuity made them wealthy, and placed a great deal of money in the hands of the men of religion who were responsible for their administration and maintenance.

Beyond the walls as a rule would be the cemetery, the 'city of the dead' where criminals might lurk out of reach of the police. At Tripoli it was so full that in places bones lay about on the surface, prompting al-Tijani to

47

Opposite: Detail of silk cloth of the thirteenth or fourteenth century, probably from Granada. By this later period, the patterns of figures in roundels had given way to designs in broad bands and geometrical interlace. The geometrical patterns were highly developed with strong line and bright colour to give textiles to match the growing elaboration of tilework and plasterwork.

Below: The Alcaiceria of Granada; the old silk market is all that remains of the souks or market streets which clustered round the Great Mosque where the cathedral now stands. The name, Al-Qaysariya, is still used at Fes for this central commercial area.

recall the headless bodies buried there after a notorious execution for treason. Executions may have taken place at the *musalla*, the 'place of prayer' also outside the walls, a large open space normally used for major festivals; in times of drought it might witness the prayer for rain. Immediately inside the walls was the space for the sheep or cattle market. Pack animals, which carried everything for a civilization without any form of wheeled transport, were similarly stabled just inside the gates, or on the ground floor of the inns or caravanserais, where merchants could live above their goods and beasts. Larger warehouses might be provided in the souks, the market streets which clustered in the centre of the city in the neighbourhood of the Great Mosque. Artificial tunnels beneath their awnings and wooden roofs or their stone vaults, their shops produced many of the goods they offered for sale: all kinds of cloth, leatherwork, metalwork, ropework, basketwork, woodwork, cosmetics and perfume. Heavier industries such as smithies, tanneries and potteries fired perhaps with the black cake of crushed olive stones produced by the oil press, might have their own districts. Food shops and markets were more widely scattered. Bakeries, in whose ovens families would leave their food to cook, were found in the quarters. The quarters might also have their own bathhouses, mosques and shrines, with churches and synagogues for the Christians and Jews. From the thirteenth century in North Africa, too late for anywhere in Andalus except Granada, appeared the splendid *madrasas* or colleges in which students of the sciences of Islam lived, worked and prayed, often by the tomb of some holy man.

The government of the city was a combination of autonomy and autocracy. In the house, where the respectable family lived in careful seclusion, the head of the family was the authority; problems of ownership, inheritance and so forth were referred to the qadi for judgment in accordance with the Law. In the quarter, the headman represented the administration. Markets were supervised by the *muhtasib*. His commission, to 'command the right and prohibit the wrong', in practice meant the enforcement of customary rules, a task for an experienced professional which varied from city to city. In theory he was responsible for thoroughfares, bathhouses, inns, the water supply and public places in general, but is unlikely to have been so important. Many of the public institutions, for example, were charities, supervised rather by the qadi and the men of religion. Over all was the governor, with his troops and police, lodged in the citadel.

The system left no room for elected councils to take corporate decisions; corporations as such were unknown. Members of a trade, often related to each other and working in the same street or quarter, were under an officer appointed by the governor. They might build themselves a mosque and turn out in a body on feast days, even for military service, but could not be described as a guild. Quarters likewise were jealous of their identity. Their young men formed gangs, which were often criminal; they too might provide contingents for the militia. The 'ulama' or scholars of the Law were highly respected. But since there were no constitutional ways in which any of these groups could decide upon the government of the city, their political activity and influence was informal. Under their leadership, the populace might help or hinder the administration to the point of riot and rebellion, joining in the making and unmaking of the despot in the citadel. These, however, were the actions of unruly subjects dissatisfied with a master they were accustomed to obey.

One reason for the lack of corporate bodies to act in the name of their

members was that such bodies were not recognized by the Islamic Law, which admitted only the rights of individuals. This stricture applied also to the family, which was seen simply as a collection of individuals in family relationships. These relationships were dealt with under different heads, rather than governed by a single rule – marriage, divorce and widowhood; concubinage and motherhood; testaments; inheritance; blood money to next of kin; and decency. Nevertheless it was the family which by custom made up for the lack of corporate bodies, acting as an economic association, a social group which gave its members a recognized place in the community and in society at large, and a political force to be reckoned with.

The family was the basic unit of production. The land was worked by households, whether the members of these households were owners or tenants. Manufactures were the work of small family concerns. Big tasks, notably in building, were put together from assignments and commissions of the kind reported for New Fes. Labour was casual, hired for the occasion; the prisoners of war at New Fes, who provided the gangs, were convenient but not essential. There certainly were slaves – white Europeans and black Africans – but they were most typically employed within the household to raise the family's standard of living or to increase its output; the industrious slave might work on his own account. In sugar plantations and factories, and in the Saharan salt mines, slaves might form a large and permanent workforce, but these were exceptional. In commerce, brothers and sons formed networks of agents stretching from city to city. Merchants expanded their business by buying and selling on commission from those with the capital to invest. They entered into partnership with each other for particular ventures, carefully calculating their contributions and their consequent share in the profits. But since these partnerships ended with the conclusion of the enterprise, nothing replaced the family.

The great merchant family made use of bonds of kinship beyond those of the individual household. The extended family, whose members all claimed descent from a common ancestor several generations back, was not always economically so important, except among nomadic peoples who migrated in tribes. Socially, however, it was highly significant, assigning to its members their position in the world. Their place in a line stretching back into the past and forward into the future was fixed by their names, Ibn, meaning 'Son of', and Abu, 'Father of'. Collectively the group was known by the prefix Banu, 'Sons of (a founding father)'. Lineage of this kind was a matter for pride and jealousy; in principle, its honour was defended by the feud, in which families revenged themselves upon each other for injuries done to their members. In places like Ghoumrassen, the feud was a method of government. Where the sultan and the qadi were in control, feuding was more of a crime, since the state provided for compensation and satisfaction in accordance with the Law. Nevertheless it might be pursued simply for the sake of prestige, or as part of the struggle of rival lineages to gain power, in the service of the ruling dynasty or even in its place.

The structure of the family was determined both by the Law and by custom. Property, for example, was minutely partitioned among the members in accordance with Islamic rules of inheritance, or maintained undivided for the group as a whole by the unwritten codes of tribal practice. In either case, the heirs and the inheritance stayed together. The head of the family, eldest son, eldest brother, exercised a general direction, sometimes a general management, not only of his own household. The men, as a rule, looked after the women's shares. The

Right: Ivory casket made to the order of the Caliph Hakam II for his concubine, the lady Subh, the mother of his son 'Abd al-Rahman. When the child died in infancy, it was her second son Hisham who succeeded to the throne under the regency of his mother and her favourite Ibn Abi 'Amir, Almanzor. Peacocks, small birds and antelopes confront each other on either side of a central stem from which the foliage branches into an all-embracing arabesque beneath the band of inscription round the rim.

Above: Ataurique or design of intertwining stems, fruits, flowers and leaves, carved in marble for the palace of the Caliph 'Abd al-Rahman III at al-Zahra' outside Cordova. In this architectural art of the tenth century, when the wealth of a great country was concentrated in the capital, expense was no obstacle to the gratification of a desire for ornamentation beyond all previous bounds. The underlying structure began to disappear as the possibilities of marble, the traditional material of luxurious building, were stretched to the limit. When the caliphate came to an end and the concentration of wealth disappeared, the taste was pursued in the cheaper but more versatile material of plaster.

position of the women was critical in this respect, for at marriage their portion of the family's wealth was transferred with them into the keeping of their husband. Marriages were therefore arranged inside the family rather than outside; the ideal pair were cousins on the male side. In this way property remained within the group. If marriages took place outside the family, they were arranged as a form of alliance between two lineages. Since women were so valuable, they were protected by fathers, brothers and husbands; their treatment was a mark of rank. The women of the poor might work outside, unveiled, as was normal in the countryside, but any family able to follow the stricture of the Law, which prohibited women from all but the most essential journeys outside the house, and from all but necessary encounters with men who were not close relatives, was careful to do so.

Slave women and concubines had more freedom, at least until they had children. I'timad al-Rumaykiya, named after her royal lover and her previous owner, won the heart of Mu'tamid at Seville when she finished the verse he had challenged his vizier to complete. In *The Collar of the Dove*, Ibn Hazm dwelt on the art and artlessness of Love as he or one of his heroes pursued the girl who took his fancy across the bridge at Cordova, or followed her through the assembled company from window to window. Such girls were often accomplished musicians and dancers; they provided the aristocracy with its pleasures as well as its passions. At one end of the scale they went on to be wives and mothers, at the other to be prostitutes. If they had been well-educated, they acted as governesses, teaching young princes poetry, calligraphy and the Koran. Some women at Cordova earned a living by copying manuscripts.

Umm, 'Mother of', was the coveted title of the wife who bore a son. For the concubine it was the ultimate achievement. Subh, 'Aurora', the mother of the Umayyad caliph Hisham II, was a Basque concubine who secured the succession for her infant son, thereby attaining a paramount influence over the affairs of state within the vast palace city of al-Zahra'. This influence, however, could be exercised only through a man – the great chamberlain Ibn Abi 'Amir, who was her protégé and chosen minister on behalf of her child. As his personal following grew, and his rivals were eliminated by strangulation, imprisonment and execution, she was pushed aside and the seat of government was transferred to his own royal city. As the omnipotent Almanzor, he hastened to found his own dynasty. But his career is a good example of the way in which patronage was required to supplement or replace the bonds of kinship.

Almanzor may have begun as the lover of the princess Subh. Patronage, however, was more often homosexual. Male homosexuality flourished in a society in which female companionship was severely restricted to certain circumstances. Male prostitutes dyed their buttocks yellow with henna; at Bijaya Ibn Tumart, the Mahdi of the Almohads, attacked them and their painted faces in the streets. Youths were ardently courted; attachments formed gave daring on the battlefield. On the base of a column from al-Zahra' appears the following inscription:

> In the name of God, the blessing of God upon the servant of God, 'Abd al-Rahman, the Commander of the Faithful. One of the things made at the hands of Shunayf, 'Little Earring', his young slave and friend, in the year three hundred and forty-two (953–4). The work of Sa'd, his servant. [2]

A privileged, wealthy boy favourite like this was not very different from the so-called 'pages' or 'young men' brought from outside the lands of Islam (where no-one might be reduced to slavery) into the households of princes. Provided with names like Jawhar, 'Jewel', Sandal, 'Sandalwood', and 'Anbar, 'Ambergris', they grew up in personal attendance on their master to form his bodyguard and to become his trusted lieutenants. Around them the prince built his retinue of slaves, freedmen and clients.

The composition of these retinues varied. Eunuchs were employed in attendance upon the women, but also in government. The slave troops of the Umayyad and Fatimid armies, the Slavs and the Blacks, were largely replaced by mercenaries. Families of viziers became established in the service of a dynasty; many were scholars. In this way patronage reached out still further. Great men in the service of the prince had their own clientèles; the scholars belonged to a wide community whose members traced their intellectual descent from their teachers as carefully as kinsmen their lineage; pupils of the same master acknowledged their affinity. By pious gifts and pious foundations, the monarch endeavoured to secure the support of this influential class, and of the people at large. Governors sent out into the provinces might escape from the orbit of the sovereign, but independent rulers might well be drawn into submission. The loyalty of the following which the prince thus attracted upheld the constitutional

Above: This perforated brass globe comes from Venice at the end of the fifteenth century. It is of a kind originally intended as an incense-burner, but employed in Europe—where examples were made by Muslim craftsmen—as a hand-warmer. The style is Syrian and Egyptian rather than Maghribi.

ideal of a covenant between the sovereign and the people which was expressed in the oath of homage received by the monarch at his accession:

And this is the admonition, to the caliph and to his officers and to the Muslim folk, which binds you to him and him to you, that he may not blast your deputations with fire, nor keep back from you anything that his government extends to you, that he may give you what you should receive, and not conceal himself from you. May God help you to fulfil your obligation, and help him in the charge of your affairs.[3]

These words were repeated in turn to each delegation as it presented itself to the new caliph Mustansir, 'Who Asks Help from God', only ten to fifteen years before the Almohad empire disintegrated. At the end of the fourteenth century, in a time of still greater turmoil, Ibn Khaldun looked back upon such reversals of fortune, and offered an explanation. Descended from an old Arab family of Seville, he was clear about the importance of blood, of the tie which bound together the offspring of a common ancestor in mutual loyalty and joint action, but gloomy about its fate. The qualities of kinship he found at their finest and fiercest in the wilderness, among the tribesmen of the mountains and the deserts who ruled themselves by their family honour; he found them at their weakest in the cities, among people who were governed like sheep. Yet the tribesmen were savage, poor and ignorant, the townsmen civilized, rich, skilful and learned. It seemed to him that it was in the nature of human society to travel from one extreme to the other, and back again; in this way civilizations came and went, their moments of greatness set between the barbarism of the past and the decadence of the future.

The pivot of the process was the state. Tribal loyalties produced conquering armies creating dynasties of noble monarchs. These ruled with justice, establishing conditions in which urban society could grow and prosper, until they succumbed to tyranny, to luxury, and to the feebleness which ensured their defeat by fresh invaders. No greater contrast could be imagined than that between the Almohads at the end of their career and the Marinids at the outset of theirs:

When Mahyu ibn Abi Bakr perished of the wounds he had received at the battle of Alarcos [in 1195], he left three sons of whom the eldest, 'Abd al-Haqq, succeeded him as leader of the Banu Marin. And 'Abd al-Haqq was the best of princes, taking charge of their welfare yet refraining from their possessions, setting them upon the right road while taking thought for what was to come. Thus their days passed. But when the fourth Almohad caliph of the west, al-Nasir, perished [in 1213] on his return from the battle of Las Navas de Tolosa, the son who took his place was a child, Yusuf al-Mustansir, whom the Almohads raised to the caliphate before the age of puberty. The strength of folly and childish desire distracted him from affairs of state and the direction of the kingdom, so that resolution was sapped and government neglected as the Almohads took advantage of the free rein he gave to their insolence, and the relaxation of the grasp of tyranny and subjection upon their necks. Thus the frontiers crumbled and the army of protection failed, while they made light of the matter, and their fair wind died away . . .[4]

This calculated rhetoric should not persuade us to accept the moral. Dynasties did not necessarily come to an end because they sank in

The remains of a water-mill below the great bridge across the Guadalquivir at Cordova. The use of water-power in this way was a natural extension of the hydraulic technology which supplied water for drinking and irrigation, and included the principle of the noria or water-wheel for the mechanical lifting and pouring of water from the river into the canals to the fields. Through the mill the water became doubly fertile, producing the flour for the bread which was synonymous with life. By the number of its mills the prosperity of the land was known.

idleness. They might well last for hundreds of years because their title was accepted by the peoples they ruled. The royal families of North Africa, apparently at the end of their allotted span in the lifetime of Ibn Khaldun, survived for at least another century, as did the states they had inherited. The society and its civilization proved still more durable. What Ibn Khaldun has to say about the economics of this civilization is more important.

Greedy and extortionate governments are bad; they make people disinclined to work, and disposed to emigrate. Those on the other hand which respect their subjects' property, like that excellent leader of the Banu Marin, 'Abd al-Haqq, provide the essential conditions for growth. Growth, according to Ibn Khaldun, is a matter of the market, the size of which depends upon the size of the population. A numerous people is able to move away from subsistence, each man for himself on the land, through specialization, each man concentrating on a particular task whose product he can sell. Development continues as crafts multiply and people congregate first in villages, then in towns, then in cities. Trade becomes elaborate, while superabundance ends in the refinement of skill and the multiplication of luxuries. The state meanwhile does more than merely protect; it accelerates the process by its expenditure, which buys from the people ever more goods and services. Provided that it can refrain from excessive taxation, it will see its revenues naturally increase from the wealth it has helped to create, and will be able to spend still more.

There is no doubt that the society created by the Arab conquests in the west was a dynamic society which grew in wealth and numbers. The economy was first stimulated by the booty and prisoners taken by the Arab raiders, then by the tribute exacted from the conquered population. It became urban as the garrison camps became permanent settlements like Kairouan, intensively agricultural as the land around was colonized and farmed to feed the new cities. It became commercial as the lines of advance by the armies became the highways of the empire, routes of trade and travel from end to end of the Muslim world and far beyond. They created and supplied a demand for commodities from the porcelain of China and the spices of the Indies to the slaves of Europe and tropical Africa. Irrigation, mining and metallurgy, ceramics, textiles, woodwork, paper, the art of calligraphy: all of them came to support, in their various ways, a larger and more sophisticated *'umran* or civilization. The state contributed to its elaboration not only by the expenditure of the revenues it received from taxation, but as a source of capital for larger works and commercial enterprises. In 955 a great ship, built at Seville, sailed for Egypt on behalf of the caliph 'Abd al-Rahman III himself, laden with money and goods for trade.

Violence, however, was never far away. It was as much a part of economics as of politics. The great ship which sailed for Egypt in 955 encountered, captured and robbed a smaller Fatimid vessel sailing from Sicily to Ifriqiya. Merchants were often pirates. War was a lucrative enterprise, whose value was calculated. The city of Mansura, which attracted merchants from all over the Maghrib, was intended to acquire the commercial fortune of the city of Tlemcen which it was built to besiege. More successful than the murdered sultan Abu Ya'qub were the Christian rulers of Spain and Sicily, who seized for themselves so much of the Muslim West. Conquest deprived its civilization of a large part of its resources. Yet even before the collapse of Andalus in the middle of the thirteenth century, there were good reasons why the impressive growth of the Muslim economy should not continue indefinitely.

From the middle of the eleventh century, the economy of western Europe expanded very much in accordance with the theory of Ibn Khaldun. This backward region, which had provided timber, slaves and furs, began to export its own manufactures in exchange for primary produce and luxuries. Its merchants seized control of trade in the Mediterranean; the sultans saw them as a lucrative source of revenue and encouraged their dealings in Muslim ports. Ifriqiya became an important supplier of wax, wool and leather to Italy, France and Aragon, while Tunis developed as a station halfway between Alexandria, Barcelona, Marseilles and Genoa. The tendency towards production for trade with the rapidly developing countries of western Europe was not confined to Islam. Sicily, under its Christian rulers, supplied grain to northern Italy, while the farmlands of Andalus, conquered by Castile, were turned over to sheep.

So far as Islam was concerned, economic dependence of this kind upon a foreign market was never total. Granada in particular retained the traditional economy of Muslim Spain with its agriculture, its manufactures and its North African commerce. In the shadow of the Christian West, however, the scope for initiative was severely restricted. Warfare alone came to offer an opportunity for new enterprise. Following the capture of Granada in 1492, Spain persecuted the Moriscoes, the remaining Spanish Muslims, until they were finally expelled in 1609. Fleeing to North Africa, many of them joined the corsairs whose attacks on Christian shipping in the sixteenth century had made Algiers into one of the largest and wealthiest cities of the Mediterranean. Isolated by the eradication of Islam from the Iberian peninsula, North Africa entered the modern world as the land of Barbary, a country in which piracy on a large scale had become the most efficient and most profitable form of economic activity.

Opposite: The projecting eaves of the Alcazar or royal palace of Seville. On their carved wooden brackets below the green tiles of the pitched roofs, they are a conspicuous, Chinese-like feature of the fourteenth century in Spain and Morocco, protecting in particular the delicate interior façades around the courts. The wood is cedar from the mountains of Spain and North Africa; the long poles from the upper branches are used in the balconies of traditional buildings in Morocco and Algeria today.

Left: Wood and ivory casket of the fourteenth century in Spain, with bronze hinges and geometrical pattern inlaid in ivory and wood. Gold floral arabesques complete a design which may be compared with the pattern of the silk fabric on page 49.

THE
MUSLIM MIND

History, for the believer, is sacred history. The scattering of the sons of Noah after the Flood has been countered by the force of revelation. The prophets of God have preached a message which has been increasingly heard and understood. Those who refused to listen have been destroyed, their place taken by those like the Jews and the Christians who have followed the messengers but remained deficient in their understanding, blind to the plain meaning. It is Muhammad (God bless him and save him!), the last and greatest of the prophets, who has finally procured acceptance of the truth. With him a new age of the world began. The community of true believers which he founded is the community of the future which, if it does not eventually reunite the whole of mankind in submission to God, will impose a simple division between the saved and the damned. Meanwhile, in accordance with God's will, that community has expanded to rule the greater part of the known world. Within its sphere, it has established a semblance of the divine order. The community governs itself by the Law of God, and dominates those of other creeds, the Jews and Christians, who live under its protection. Beyond its borders, on the other hand, this happy state of affairs gives way to disorder in which Christians and even pagans, total unbelievers, rule. It is a pious duty to wage war upon this unnatural condition, to reduce it as far as possible to obedience.

The attitude of the true believer, therefore, is one of unquestioned superiority. It is justified by the Law of God, the divine dispensation which governs the universe. So far as humanity is concerned, this Law is contained in the revelation of God to Muhammad. The Prophet, the Messenger of God, received it over a period of more than twenty years in the form of pronouncements which he duly uttered, and which were then memorized and written down. The book which God thus gave to His community, the Qur'an or Koran, 'that which is to be read', became its chief treasure. As the very Word of God, the Book vindicated God's truth in the face of indifference and rejection:

> Those who do not believe the words of God, and unrighteously kill the prophets, and kill those of the people who command justice, preach them an agonizing punishment;[1]

The 'nave' of the Great Mosque of Kairouan, running from the porch to the mihrab in the far south wall, an orientation common to all the early mosques of North Africa and Spain. To the right of the mihrab is the original wooden pulpit. The chandeliers are flat brass rings with holes through which glass oil lamps hung.

while those who have faith and do good work, God will cause to enter

> gardens beneath which rivers run; they will be allowed bracelets of gold and pearl, and their clothes will be of silk.[2]

The fullness of the Law which it proclaimed was spelled out at length in a supplementary revelation, the sayings of Muhammad himself, his decisions and his acts, which together form his Sunna, his Custom. By this Custom the early community lived, and by it the community of the faithful has lived ever since.

The Sunna was a matter for enormous pride, and intense humility. To have God's Law was to stand at the summit of creation but nevertheless to understand the distance between that position and perfection. Pride saw the heavenly ideal in the earthly reality. The poet Ibn Rashiq, addressing the great city of Kairouan, declared:

> How many were in her of nobles and gentles, white of face and proud of right hand, joining in worship and obedience to God in thought and deed; a school of all excellences, pouring out its treasure to lord and people; men of God who brought together the sciences of religion and burnished all the usages of Tradition and the problems of the Koran; doctors who, if you asked them, rolled away the clouds with their knowledge of the Law, their pure language and their explanations. . . . Kairouan was reckoned according to them when the number of its pulpits was the flower of the land; she shone above Egypt as she boasted of them, and ran above Baghdad . . .[3]

But the past tense is significant. Ibn Rashiq was lamenting 'the punishment of God', the ruin of its civilization when the city was abandoned by the sultan and many of its people in 1057, and fell prey to plunderers. In the language of humility his fellow poet Ibn Sharaf said: 'The sins of Kairouan have outgrown forgiveness, although God forgives.'

Sin of some kind was in fact unavoidable. Of necessity, the reality fell short of the ideal. The Law itself in all its heavenly perfection, a complete set of rules governing every detail of human conduct, could never be fully known on earth, however hard the scholars might try. The four schools of the Law, each slightly different in its teaching from the others, were an acknowledgment of the fact. Despite the collective wisdom of the learned, in every case presented for judgment or simply for an opinion, there was an element of doubt, a small margin of error. The margin widened to infinity when the Law was set aside as too inconvenient for the purposes of government, economy and society, and man-made rules were adopted. This universal practice, almost invariably condoned by the jurists as a sad necessity in a wicked world, made for a poor approximation to the model. However carefully it had preserved the revelation of God to Muhammad, the community was very far from that of the golden age of the Prophet.

The imperative remained; 'Serve God!' – the Koran is explicit. What was required was a constant effort, first to learn and then to do. God, said Ibn Abi Zayd in the preface to his *Risala* or 'Letter', has taught man what he did not know, granting him an immense favour. It is necessary that this knowledge be fixed in the mind as durably as an engraving in stone. For this reason Ibn Abi Zayd composed his epistle in answer to a request for guidance, setting out the basic elements of the Law according to the Malikites for use in school. The work became the standard introduction

'What God has given to me is greater than what He has given to you . . .' Koran, Sura XXVII (The Ant), verses 36–9. Sulayman (Solomon), advancing at the head of his armies, of genies, men and birds, rejects the gifts of the Queen of Sheba, who worships the sun. With the power over created things which God has given him, so that the ant runs underground at his approach, he threatens her with overwhelming defeat and submission; a genie will bring him her throne before he can rise from his place. The page is from a twelfth-century Koran, written in the characteristic script of the Maghrib, which developed independently in North Africa and Spain. The roundels in the text mark the beginning and the end of each verse; the design in the margin grew from a stylized tree or plant symbolic of the eternal Garden to which the lines of the sacred words direct the believer.

to the subject. Its author was a native of Spain who in the tenth century became one of the leading jurists of Kairouan. His preface continues: let the child learn what the tongue should say, the heart believe and the limbs do, whether it be absolutely necessary, over and above what is strictly required, or simply desirable. God will help the believer to perform this lifelong duty to his creator, provided he has faith, and does not try to go beyond the prescribed limits. These two conditions are inseparable; together they amount to trust. The seal of Hakam I was engraved with the words: 'Hakam puts his faith in God, and clings to Him'; that of his son 'Abd al-Rahman II declared: ''Abd al-Rahman is content with God's decree.'

Without such confidence, man, it was believed, could do nothing. With it, he could go forward with God's help along the road to Paradise. The monarchs of the Umayyad dynasty conform in the literature to an ideal type. Brave and resolute, wise, virtuous and just, they wield their power in the name of Islam to overcome the infidel and bring the heavenly order to earth. 'Abd al-Rahman I requires obedience from the rebel as God requires it from His creatures; he has brought civilization out of desolation. Hisham is willing to set aside his throne should the qadi give judgment against him. Hakam is the instrument of fate, dealing their appointed deaths to rebels and infidels, leaving the country like a soft and comfortable bed. It is rare to find, after the standard eulogy, an opinion

like that about 'Abd Allah, that for all his piety he was mean and murderous.

Such obedience to a stern command had its reward. The Garden of Heaven would open to receive the Muslim, the man or woman who submitted wholeheartedly to the will of God. On earth, the Law was not meant simply as an obligation. It was the means to the full life for which God had intended His creatures. God, said Ibn Abi Zayd, had brought man forth from the womb into His gentleness, to enjoy what He had provided. For this He had revealed the Law. To do right was to do well. To do well was to do properly and successfully. Yusuf ibn Tashfin, in his conquest of Spain, was careful to consult the jurists at every step for legal opinions about the actions he had in mind. Ordinary Muslims sought guidance in more humble matters: for instance, was the husband who divorced his wife and was therefore obliged to let her take away the 200 gold pieces he had given her as a dowry entitled to deduct the 150 gold pieces which, by custom, he should have received from her father as a contribution to the cost of the wedding? For every dispute, said a proverb, there is a solution in the Law.

Those in search of a remedy were wise to avoid the sultan, who had a summary way with complaints. The qadi might be approached more safely. Appointed by the ruler to judge in accordance with the Law, the qadi dealt with contracts, inheritances and family affairs, matters of decency and so on in which the state had no urgent administrative or financial interest. At the same time he was the recognized guardian of the Law as the supreme authority, a censor of morals ready to denounce the evils of society, whoever the offender might be. At Kairouan the Qadi Ibn Ghanim lectured the Aghlabid amir on the injustice of his rule. At Cordova the Qadi al-Baluti reprimanded the caliph 'Abd al-Rahman III for covering a roof of the palace of al-Zahra' with silver and gold. On this position as keeper of the community's conscience his reputation rested.

Like the Law, however, the stern face of the qadi could smile. Al-Khushani's *History of the Judges of Cordova*, written in the tenth century, emphasizes the benevolence which flows from a severe attachment to the right. The good judge was generous in the full sense of the word, giving all possible help to those who came to him with a problem, whether it was simply good advice or more material assistance. He could afford not to see the drunk in the street, and to indulge a little impropriety in his own behaviour. Muhammad ibn Bashir dressed in the height of fashion; al-Baluti's well-known wit invited the facetious question: 'Where is the fault in a virgin who has gone to bed with the boys for the good of their souls?' The problem, he answered primly, did not arise in the doctrine of his school.

Away from the towns, in the countryside where people managed their affairs by village and clan with only occasional intervention from above, the man of God was equally respected, and still more important. For such communities the feud, an eye for an eye and a tooth for a tooth, was often the only guarantee of respect for persons and property ruled by customs sometimes remote from the Law of Islam. The Muslim sage, settled among them or simply passing by, was welcome as an arbitrator, one who could stop a quarrel before whole families had wiped each other out.

The courtyard of the Great Mosque of Kairouan, looking towards the prayer-hall. The dome above the main entrance to the hall is matched by the dome above the mihrab at the back. Built in the ninth century, the mosque was a vast meeting-place where the scholars of the Law taught their pupils in the colonnades; a cistern beneath the courtyard collected rainwater for the city's supply.

When two villages of the Sahel, the east coast of Tunisia, began to fight about the boundary between them, the shaykh al-Jadidi hurried to insist on an arrangement. Two men of the first village had been killed, but only one of the second, which was told to pay compensation for the extra victim. After grumbling, the villagers agreed; and the boundary was duly marked.

In cases like this, the Law withdrew behind the representative of the Law. The advice he gave might be more in accordance with the spirit than the letter, but his authority was all the greater for being less specific. Ibn Yasin, going down into the Sahara to abolish the old ways, and to force the desert tribesmen to stand by the discipline of the Law in his Almoravid regiments, was exceptional. The tendency was to equate the man with the religion and to see, not a prophet calling to repentance, nor yet a vigilant supervisor, but a source of spiritual power to bless a familiar way of life. The activities of the holy man helped that way of life to continue from day to day; his presence ensured its continuation from year to year.

This was universally true. In a world of imperfection, the Muslim survived by the grace and goodness of God. Helped by the Almighty, under the guidance of His scholars and His saints, he could feel that whatever he did was essentially right, from eating, drinking and sleeping to waking and working, buying and selling, commanding and serving. The ways of the community were the true ways, confidently attributed to Islam even when they did not derive directly from its commandments. In a very important sense, the faith was how people lived. The familiar behaviour which every member of the society was brought up to expect of the others, men and women, rich and poor, townsmen and countrymen, was the product of belief and its outward sign. This behaviour was measured by the common routine, the celebration of the hours of the day, the days of the week, the weeks of the month, the months of the year, the years of the life, as God's time flowed onwards to

The great clock of the Marinid sultan Abu 'Inan, constructed in 1357 at Fes outside the Bou Anania, the madrasa which he founded and which bears his name. The thirteen bronze bells upon their wooden brackets seem to have been struck with weights let down from the ends of the beams projecting overhead, which once supported an over-hanging roof. Doors in the windows behind are said to have opened as the clock chimed. The mechanism is unknown, but it was probably a clepsydra or water-clock worked by water running from a higher to a lower level. The strange ruin has become known as the House of the Magician, since according to legend the clock was owned and worked by the magic of a Jewish sorcerer at Meknes; alternatively, it was silenced by a Jewish wizard, whose wife had miscarried at the sound of its bells.

eternity: 'By the working of this machine to watch the hours, may God prolong the life of the city and perpetuate its landmarks.' The inscription comes from the palace of the Norman King Roger II at Palermo in the twelfth century, but is in Arabic, and is wholly Muslim in sentiment.

The day, which ran from sunset to sunset, was punctuated by the five times of prayer. The week culminated in the midday prayer on Friday, for which the congregation assembled in the principal mosque to hear the sermon in the name of the reigning monarch. The month went strictly by the moon, a visible reminder of its passing. Twelve of them made the lunar year of 354 days, dated from 622 AD, when Muhammad left Mecca for Medina, and marked by the fast of the ninth month, Ramadan. In the twelfth and last occurred the great pilgrimage to Mecca. Moving slowly backwards through the seasons of the solar year, these great occasions and their festivals separated themselves from the natural times of sowing and reaping, mating and breeding, travelling and staying at home. They carried the faithful onwards from childhood to the inevitable moment of death:

> In the name of God, the Compassionate, the Merciful! May He bless and save the Prophet Muhammad and his family!
> Say: He is the One God, God the Lord, neither begetting nor begotten; there is none like Him.
> Say: it is tremendous tidings, from which you turn away!
> This is the grave of 'Atiya, son of 'Abdun, the tailor, who died on Tuesday in the second ten days of the month of Jumada (the First or Second) in the year 432 (January–February 1041), witnessing that there is no god but God, and Muhammad is the Servant of God and His Messenger.[4]

The reward of this humble citizen of Kairouan was in heaven. His fellows remained in the comfort of the Law on earth. Sure of God's Word, they might hope for the best. At the same time, they might fear the worst. 'The punishment of God' which emptied Kairouan a few years later was a reminder of the fundamental uncertainty of this life. The mill, said Ibn Sharaf, had turned upon its pole, fiercely grinding all that fell beneath. It is necessary, Ibn Abi Zayd had declared a hundred years earlier, to believe in the predestination of evil as well as good, of bitterness as well as sweetness, by divine decree. It was inconceivable that it should be otherwise. God is too great for anything to exist, or anything to happen, except in accordance with His will and foreknowledge. Although in Islam mankind lived at a higher level than ever before, the realization of this immense power and its consequences was correspondingly profound. Compared to God, the world is of no account:

> Know that the life of the world is only play, entertainment and outward show, and boasting among yourselves, and competition in wealth and children, like plants after rain which delight the grower, then wither, so that you see them yellow and turn to sticks and straws.[5]

Such passages of the Koran did not prevent a special prayer, for instance, for rain. Yet the bridge over the Guadalquivir, the 'Great River' of Cordova, was frequently broken by the floods, while droughts left the harvests to perish. It was accepted as God's will: 'No affliction strikes in the earth or in yourselves but it is in a Book before We bring it into being.' It was written.

Marble relief from the Fatimid fortress city of Mahdia, depicting the monarch with a musician playing to him on a form of pipe. The sovereign sits cross-legged, in state; his crown is a bonnet of soft material pulled into three peaks above a diadem which even in the sculpture was once set with precious stones. Across his belted robe runs the woven inscription called tiraz; the glass of wine which he holds in his hand was a symbol of power and sovereignty unconnected with the drinking of alcohol, for which the aristocracy was frequently denounced. On the wooden ceiling of the Cappella Palatina in the royal palace of Palermo, painted for Roger II of Sicily by Fatimid artists from Egypt, the king is depicted in the same posture, with the same crown.

The poets exaggerated the heights of prosperity and the depths of disaster. But they had cause. Andalus, rich and fertile, walked precariously between the perils of empire, internal disorder and foreign invasion. The hegemony of Cordova was maintained by continual warfare at home and abroad, the outcome of which was never certain. It called for atrocity, mobs slaughtered, armies annihilated, roads lined with the crosses of the crucified, the city surrounded by heads stuck on spikes. The nervous effort mocked the splendours of al-Madinat al-Zahra', the Radiant City, and led 'Abd al-Rahman III to declare at the end of his life that he had known only fourteen days entirely without care. Only by constant endeavour was the vision of harmony upheld with any semblance of success for two hundred and fifty years.

With 'Abd al-Rahman III, the Caliph al-Nasir li-Din Allah, 'Victorious for the Faith', providence seemed genuinely to reward the faithful. The fires of discord, said the chronicler, were quenched, the body politic cured of its sickness. Like the new moon he came to inaugurate his reign; growing to the full, he watched the blessings of God continue to increase. Victories were complete, rejoicing general; powerful was Islam, happy the human race, fortunate the time. The golden age of the past returned.

Yet within fifty years of his death, the power he had created had vanished. In 1013 the poet Ibn Hazm fled from the sack of Cordova by the Berbers, returning years later to lament the passing of its splendour:

> I stood upon the ruins of our house, its traces wiped out, its signs erased, its familiar spots vanished. Decay had turned its cultivated bloom to sterile waste. In savagery after society, ugliness after beauty, wolves howled and devils played in the haunts of ghosts and dens of wild beasts that once had been luxuriant and melodious. Men like swords, damsels like dolls, overflowing with riches beneath an ornamentation so palatial it reminded you of heaven, all were scattered with the change of time. Those elegant apartments, the plaything of destruction, were wilder now than the gaping mouths of lions, announcing the end of the world, revealing the fate of its inhabitants . . . [6]

Such changes of fortune, vividly expressed in this high-flown imagery, made for real, deep-seated anxiety. The good Muslim denounced the hypocrite, the man who pretended to be what he was not, God-fearing and Law-abiding, like those men of Medina who long ago had tried to conceal from Muhammad their hostility to his message. The hypocrites were the covert infidels whom the Muslims of Spain saw hidden in the heart of Andalus, threatening to bring down its civilization more surely than its open enemies, the Christians of the north. The one might shade into the other. When the fortress of Bobastro was eventually taken, ten years after the death of the celebrated rebel 'Umar ibn Hafsun, the tomb was opened in the presence of the caliph, and the body found lying on its back in the Christian manner. The terrible secret thus revealed, the bones were exhumed and exhibited on a high pole at the gate of Cordova as a grim warning, to the delight of the faithful.

Such gestures were immensely significant. They satisfied a craving for certainty. Vileness was affirmed, right vindicated, when a bandit was crucified between a pig and a dog. At the same time they were portentous, eagerly seized upon for the future. It was a happy hour when, at the beginning of the reign of 'Abd al-Rahman III, the first head of a rebel was sent in. Conversely, when at the outset of his abominable career Ibn Hafsun took so many fortresses with so few men and so little money,

66

it was a sign of God's wrath with His people for hardness of heart and inclination to evil.

Dreams were ominous. A good dream boded well; it was sent from God. A bad dream called for spitting three times to the left, and a prayer to ward off the harm. Their interpretation needed care and skill, but they could convey the divine command, not to speak of a reprimand. An officious disciple was rapped painfully over his knuckles by the Prophet in his sleep, for having tried to keep the street urchins away from his master in the market. A favoured few enjoyed the gift of prophecy, especially when future greatness was in store. Before the revolution which overthrew the Umayyad dynasty in the east, his great-uncle Maslama at Damascus prophesied that the young 'Abd al-Rahman, the boy with two curls on his forehead, would revive the fortunes of the dynasty in the west. When the governor of Kairouan learned of the prophecy and wished to kill the fugitive prince, it was pointed out to him that he could not alter what had been decreed. And those about to die were notoriously second-sighted. At his execution the Christian martyr Perfectus correctly predicted that the royal favourite Nasr would die within the year. But by far the most common kind of prediction was by the stars.

The watching of the skies to discover the workings of fate was taken over by Muslims from the Greeks and Romans. The Koran declares that 'the heavens and earth are signs for the believers'. The chronicles therefore record the floods, earthquakes, hurricanes and lightning, the

Right: 'On the final squares the pawns become the queens' (Ibn Sharaf, Banderas, 106). Chess set of the thirteenth or fourteenth century.

eclipses (for which there was a special prayer) and the rarer celestial phenomena. Meanwhile the astrologers, the men of the stars, made their regular calculations, as in the Muslim story of Abraham. Before the birth of Abraham, Nimrod was informed by them of the coming of one who was to destroy the old religion; Nimrod, like Herod after him, killed all the new-born, but the infant naturally escaped. The tale is ambivalent; the astrologers and their science seem pagan and hostile, at best neutral, but on the other hand their information is correct. Ibn Abi Zayd in the *Risala* is explicit: it is forbidden to study the stars except to determine the direction of prayer and the hours of the night. Almanzor was violently opposed to the practice, along with philosophical studies of all kinds. The wretched Muhammad ibn Abi Jum'a, who foretold the end of his regime, had his tongue cut out before execution and crucifixion – at which, says the chronicler, all tongues were dumb. But the episode attests the great man's belief and fear. Others were less defiant, and more prudent. It was normal to consult the stars at critical times. When the sultan Abu Yusuf planned the foundation of New Fes in 1276, the two astrologers who cast the horoscope were indispensable. The precaution was wise; misfortune might equally well be written in the stars:

> *Behold a king yesterday absorbed in pleasure,*
> *judge then his kingdom with woe and war;*
> *See now the sun in the scales of Libra dropping,*
> *out of his fortune's delightful Tower.*[7]

(The Tower or House being one of the twelve divisions of the horoscope, corresponding to the twelve successive arrangements of the heavens through which the sun passed in the course of the year; in this case, the Tower is characterized by the sign of Virgo, the pagan Venus, goddess of Love.) The astrologer was therefore highly placed; the profession was fit for the finest intelligence. In the eleventh century it was represented by no less a person than the chancellor of Ifriqiya, Ibn Abi 'l-Rijal, and subsequently by a series of distinguished mathematicians.

The good Muslim, who believed in predestination, was obliged to think that to attend to the heavens in this way was simply to glimpse

Left: 'The torment of a terrible Day . . . bearing down upon their valleys' (Koran XLVI, 21, 24). Sandstorm in the Sahara.

God's will, and that those who acted on what they saw in the stars did no more than they were fated to do. The conviction of Nimrod, and of the governor of Kairouan, that the knowledge gained could be used to avert what was bound to happen, was a dangerous fallacy. Astrology was nevertheless a means of reassurance, anxiously employed, which came perilously near to beliefs of a different kind. Almanzor, making such a terrible example of the miserable astrologer, was attempting to abolish the predicted evil along with its source, the man whose utterance had brought it into being. In the eyes of the superstitious, the man of the stars became a sorcerer, a worker of magic. The black art was recognized by the Law, which punished it with death, repentance notwithstanding. Against it, charms and appropriate spells might be used, taking refuge in God, and going so far as to employ verses from the Koran and other works of sacred literature. Such verses might be written out and hung in amulets round the neck. Precautions and remedies of this kind shaded off into medicine, since sickness was the chief affliction to be feared from witchcraft. Much was to be attributed to the Evil Eye, a maleficent power in the look which some people possessed, and which they might use wittingly or unwittingly. To undo the effect of the Eye, the eyer was required to wash and throw the water over the victim. But these small matters were as nothing compared to the legendary abilities of the wizard. Morocco, which became famous for the miracles of its holy men, wrought by divine grace, acquired from these a more dubious reputation as the land of magicians, home of Aladdin's wicked uncle.

The theme of Aladdin's story, of course, is not so much the skill of the sorcerer as the access obtained to the immeasurably greater powers of the spirit world. The genie who came when the lamp was rubbed was one of numberless beings disposed to both good and evil, merging into the angels above them and the devils below. The angels surrounded the throne of God to carry out His commands, descending as guardians, two for every human being. The devils were likewise appointed one for each person, to tempt him from the way. Some, like the genies, had strength to move buildings and mountains. Their intervention in the life of the material world was only to be expected. When al-Shaytan, the Devil himself, tempted the caliph to gild the roof of his palace, the battle between good and evil was, according to the Qadi al-Baluti, in the human mind. When the poets peopled the ruins of cities and the wastes of the desert with demons, they were plundering their hoard of metaphor. But a look at traditional Muslim beliefs reported from Morocco in the twentieth century, gives some idea of the popular conceptions behind the dogmas and the fancies of the past.

The earth is supposedly inhabited by spirits who dwell especially in lonely and abandoned places. They may take the form of cats, dogs, goats and mules, sometimes people, and are a constant menace to life and limb, attacking, beating, killing, stealing away. It is wise to be on guard against them, especially at dead of night, and to propitiate them with gifts of food. Some, especially the genies of the house, are well-disposed if treated properly, but others are always wicked. They afflict with disease, and take possession of the body, requiring exorcism. An unfinished house at Marrakesh is cursed by the devil walled up in the well. Some, however, are more constructive. The tower of the Kutubiya mosque at Marrakesh was built by two genies to such a height that Mecca could be seen from the top; but then a demon in the form of a bird drove it down like a peg into the ground with blows of its wings.

Of the more elaborate legends, several display most if not all of the typical features of Islam in the west as they appear in the record from the

Top: The Moors fight on over the bodies of the fallen against their more heavily armoured opponents; a detail of frescoes of the conquest of Majorca.

Below: the hand of Fatima, an ancient symbol of good luck and protection against the evil eye, guards the house of which it is the doorknocker in the old city of Fes.

ninth century onwards. In the tale of the Oum-er-Rebia, a river of central Morocco, an evil genie blocked the source with a huge rock. The Sultan of Morocco, who was concerned to restore the natural order, learned by his skill in magic that the spring would only be released when forty wise men laid down their lives. He therefore assembled the scholars of Morocco and asked for forty of their number. But they replied that they were not the men he wanted, since their knowledge came only from books. The men required were those whose wisdom came from inspiration, the poets and the holy men, in whom flowed the divine grace. When these were summoned by the sultan, however, they also declined. Only the saintly Sidi Rahal came forward, declaring that he would overcome the genie by himself. He went to the spring, and with certain incantations so terrified the evil spirit that it fled without a fight. The spring burst out, and with his stick the man of God guided the water to the sea. Nevertheless he prophesied that the water would be barren, and that crops and gardens would never be helped by it. Meanwhile his fellow men of divine inspiration had been shamed, and had followed him to the source, where they began to pray below the great rock which blocked it. When the genie fled and the spring gushed forth, the rock fell on them and killed them all, so that the fate foreseen by the sultan was accomplished. Ever since, the Oum-er-Rebia has required its forty victims, which is why so many are drowned in the river, and why it is dangerous to bathe. Through many other similar tales, a way of life is both explained and confirmed.

Eventually, all may indeed be well, as life runs on between the heights of heaven and the depths of human perversity and ignorance. But for Muslims fate punishes as well as rewards, and the only certainty is death and judgment. For them faith is the only hope, for God knows best; only He is eternal – to Him and unto Him we return.

Lions pounce upon gazelles on the side of the Alhambra Basin, a rectangular marble trough of the mid-eleventh century from Granada. Framed by ducks and fish, they are the characteristic ornament of the period for the tank which held water for ordinary use in the palace. The motif comes from the Ancient Near East; together with the accompanying theme of eagles and griffins which occur on the short sides of this basin, it is also found carved in ivory upon the round caskets made for members of the royal family at al-Zahra'.

THE
ARAB MIND

*The central shaft of the Tower of the Infantas.
Away from the main complex of the Royal
Palace, this isolated tower in the northern
wall of the Alhambra was converted in the
middle of the fifteenth century into a pavilion,
it is said, for three princesses, two of whom
eloped with captive Christian knights. Inside
the thick masonry of the fortress are long
rooms on two floors around a tall well.
Overhead hangs the star-shaped lantern of
the ceiling, a dome of wood from which
depend the stalactites of carved plaster which
are the glory of the Alhambra. Composed of
individual prismatic shapes assembled and
cut to fit the space, these stalactites have lost
any function they once had in brick and
stone as structural elements of a vault.
Instead they coat the cheap and fragile
structures of this palatial architecture in an
art of magnificent illusion.*

*Al-ḥamdu lillāh rabb al-ʿālamīn
Al-raḥmān al-raḥīm mālik yawm al-dīn
Iyyāka naʿbudu wa iyyāka nastaʿīnu
Uhdinā al-ṣirāṭ al-mustaqīm*

*Praise to the One God, Lord of the worlds,
The compassionate, the merciful, the master of the
        Day of Judgment;
We worship You, we ask your help;
Vouchsafe to us the straight way.*[1]

So begins the Koran. The language is Arabic, the language of the sacred
scripture, the language of God Himself. As an essential part of the sacred
text, the sonorous phraseology was, for the believer, wonderful beyond
compare. No sounds could be more beautiful in their endless chant. The
literal meaning of the words was lost in their perfection. Reduced to
writing, their shapes were an insight into the eternal. No forms could
excel the patterns of their letters, squarely set down in gold on blue,
roundly described in black and white, densely interwoven. They took the
place of any sacred image. Through the ear and through the eye, the
Arabic of the Book filled the mind with the divine harmony.

Those who spoke the language as their native speech were clearly
blessed. Wisdom, it was said, had descended upon the hands of the
Chinese, the brains of the Greeks and the tongues of the Arabs. The Arabs
had received the greatest gift. Their eloquence was the proof of their
mission to the world. Before the coming of Islam it had been apparent in
their poetry, the excellence of which was the natural product of their
genius. The classic compositions of the Time of Ignorance marked them
out for the supreme revelation, for the Knowledge they would bring to
the whole world. Since the moment of truth in the lifetime of the
Prophet, these pagan odes had taken a place second only to the Koran as
examples of the heavenly beauty. They were an integral part of the
canon, scrutinized in all their complexity for the subtle secrets of their
wording by linguists whose science was part of religion itself. The
continued production of such poetry, at the less exalted level of those for
whom the golden age of the Prophet was further and further in the past,
was clear evidence of God's continued favour.

The form of the verse remained unchanged. The lines, each one
divided into two halves, were governed in each poem by a single rhythm

and a single rhyme. The rhythm was chosen from a basic five: 'Perfect',
'Ample', 'Long', 'Wide' and 'Light'. The rhyme meant that each line
ended with the same letter, a requirement calling for feats of ingenuity in
poems which might be hundreds of lines in length. The ingenuity
displayed was the measure of excellence; the finished work was indeed, as
the Arabs claimed, unique.

The content was basically that of the *qasida*, the early Arabian ode.
Qasida has the meaning of travelling towards a goal, appropriately, for
the movement of the classical poem towards its climax centred on the
celebration of a journey across the desert. The tale of this journey in
search of a lost love, evoking the heroic ardour of the beduin warrior in
separate passages strung together like the gems in a rope of pearls, offered
a highly artificial introduction to the final subject, commonly the praise of
some noble patron. With the growth of Arab civilization, the repertoire
of the qasida was enlarged to include the adventures of a courtly urban
life; these adventures became the subject of individual poems very much
shorter than the full-blown ode. The imagery of the desert, however, was
never forgotten, and the qasida itself was retained. By taking the extracts
and fragments which are often all that has survived, it is possible to
illustrate something of the range of subject-matter. By arranging these
fragments in the order in which their topics might have occurred in a
full-length ode, it is possible to give an idea of the qasida itself.

The classical ode began with a vision of desolation as the poet returned to lament the abandonment of the encampment where his beloved had dwelt. For the poets of the Muslim West, the image might be that of the ruined city:

> The empty houses stand, neglected brides
>   who hide their secrets underneath the veil.
> Behold the black night comes, and loneliness
>   gains strength as hearts begin to fail;
> No lamps except the stars until
>   the murky glooms their glimmerings curtail;
> The dust in passing trails along its cloak,
>   no sweeper but the tresses of the gale;
> A shout lives on and on; perhaps it is
>   the graves from time to time that utter in a wail.[2]

To the exiled the city itself has become the beloved, lost and gone:

> Oh Qayrawan, would I were a bird
>   to see you with the eager eye's desire;
> Oh that a sigh might soothe the burning of a heart
>   consumed by passion's fervent, longing fire.[3]

But the past is dead, returning only as a spirit in a dream to trouble the grey-haired poet with the memory of his youth.

Youth was a time of sensuous pleasure, when the poet lived the life celebrated in his verse. The exquisite charm of the desert maiden

Above: The sands of the Sahara, in the region of Sijilmasa. High as mountains, the dunes flowed in the legendary River of Sand across the path of Dhu'l-Qarnayn, Alexander the Great, as he made his way westwards towards the fabled city of Brass in the land of the setting sun. His Arabic name, 'The Man with Two Horns', derives from his historical visit to the temple of Zeus Ammon in the oasis of Siwa, west of the Nile, where he identified himself with the ram-headed god — a deity both Greek, Egyptian and Libyan. In the legendary cycle of the Arabic romance, he is an epic figure whose journeys to the ends of the earth take on the character of man's quest for God in the time before Islam.

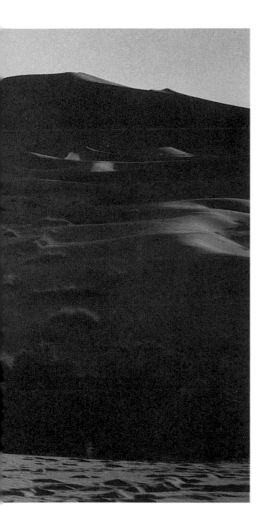

recollected in the midst of the wilderness by the hero of the classical ode induced the erotic mood:

> Beneath your eyelids is bewitchment,
>   upon your slender bough the moon is round;
> Your eyes two swords unsheathing
>   compel obedience to your command;
> The blushing of your cheeks for lovers
>   is celebrated by them through the land;
> The partings of your limbs and body
>   are like the partings of the dunes of sand;
> I'd say I saw a mouth or matching
>   pearls arranged in order in a strand;
> How should I praise your waist, however,
>   when there's no waist my praises to confound? [4]

A boy lacked the curves, but was equally desirable:

> The promised beard eventually came
>   and brought perfection to your loveliness;
> Beauty found aid, the more since, as it grew,
>   it grew inclined towards your lovers' amorousness;
> Let lust learn longing from your body's length,
>   the heart find there the way to gloriousness!
> Your face is not concealed by this new charm,
>   but brightly clad in its embroidered dress;
> Praise be to Him who gave you second grace,
>   and thirdly vigour from your comeliness. [5]

Right: Harpies or birds with human heads perch upon the backs of lions within the roundels of this silk fabric of about the year 1100 from al-Andalus; men, conceivably dressed in long coats of mail, contend with griffins in the circular border. Within the smaller rings which link the larger circles in the overall pattern, inscriptions claim that the material was made in, or for, Baghdad, presumably to deceive the customer. The fabric, of which this is a detail, was in fact found in the tomb of San Pedro de Osma, d. 1109, in the cathedral of Burgo de Osma on the Duero in Old Castile. It is a good example of the way in which so many of these Islamic textiles have survived as treasures of the Christian church. Neither their Muslim origin nor their habitually Muslim inscriptions stood in the way of their ecclesiastical use.

New beards were not usually so appreciated. Nevertheless, while it lasted, love was delicious:

> My night was blissful, for she came;
>> beauty embraced me to the break of day;
> My shoulder bore the swordbelt of her arms;
>> mine at her hips in a girdle lay.[6]

Torment, alas, was never far:

> This breath is not released by breathing's rise and fall,
>> but rather by a last long tortured gasp set free;
> No nearness gives me life, no distance death;
>> no separation to distract, no fortitude for me;
> I welcomed suffering, for the meeting brought my pain
>> a little ease; but where can Ayyub be?[7]

A joke might pass it off:

> Broad buttocks from her slender waist are hung
>> to agonize us both, myself and her;
> They pain me when I even think of them;
>> they ache as getting up she tries to stir.[8]

Better a carefree attitude; wine, mixed with water, was the way to enjoy love and everything else:

> The light of dawn is clearing in my eyes;
>> pour wine for me before the call to prayer;
> The water blending with it scatters pearls
>> that rise and float to vanish in the air;
> Drink up with the boys, of birth and breeding true,
>> and in the scents of dirty stories share;
> While liquor drunk from cheeks of young gazelles
>> brings out the roses and the jasmin fair.[9]

Above: Grapes and wine adorn an ivory inlay from a piece of furniture of the Fatimid period.

The fragrance of the flowers lingered on. The Arabs were connoisseurs of perfume, which pervaded their thoughts as well as the air they breathed. The violence of centuries was distilled into *The Sweet Smell of the Bough of Andalus the Fresh and Tender* by al-Maqqari, the last great historian of Muslim Spain, who wrote after Muslim Spain itself had disappeared. Like its people, however, the poet was doomed to depart. The imagery of the nomadic life, as the camels bear away the women high in the howdahs on their backs, gives the sense of loss. Jealousy provides an erotic touch:

> And when we stopped upon the morning of farewell,
>> dashed to the ground what once was mine to hold,
> I looked upon the litters which contained
>> the full moons hidden by their veils of gold;
> Behind the veils the curling tresses snaked
>> upon the rosy cheeks within their fold;
> At peace with those whose faces they caressed,
>> like asps they stung the heart that grief made cold.[10]

The serpent had been the most splendid riding beast on earth before it conveyed the Devil into the Garden of Eden. It was therefore especially

appropriate that it should represent the misery of this setting out, coming in its new and sexually suggestive form to ravish away the maiden from her lover. The journey once begun, and the travellers committed to the wilderness, the creature became overtly fiendish:

> But when the desert clutched them, time and fate
> aimed at them other missiles, quickening their tears;
> From snakes and serpents armed with crooked fangs
> came twisting arrows, writhing darts and spears;
> Inhabiting the waste, alone, apart,
> sharp piercing devils rose about their ears.[11]

Such viciousness was easily extended to fit, for example, the war galley with its flickering oars:

> As if the snakes had lived within the hull
> since Noah brought them when the Flood was sprung,
> The sight of heaving water rising round
> drew from each hôle a darting serpent's tongue.[12]

The sea was quite as dangerous as the desert, and just as likely to be crossed. Landsmen could only hope and pray:

> A floating speck misplaced upon the deep,
> we trusted not to drown when all else sank;
> Nine souls were we, between us and our death
> the flimsy patching of a little wooden plank.[13]

The storm that broke over the poet was the climax of his sufferings. At the same time it brought new life to the thirsty land:

> Each flower a mouth which in the gloom
> gaped at the swollen nipples of the sky;
> In grandeur marched the regiments of clouds,
> black soldiers bright with golden armoury.[14]

Below: Cordova from the Guadalquivir. It is seen here downstream from the great bridge which leads from the tower on the right to the mihrab wall of the Great Mosque on the north bank, to the left. The skyline of the large, low building is broken by the cathedral built in the sixteenth century in the middle of the vast prayer-hall. Further left stands the Alcazar or citadel of Cordova. Beginning in the eighth century as the residence of the governor by the side of the mosque where the army of the faithful assembled and prayed, the Alcazar developed under 'Abd al-Rahman I as a royal palace, keeping its importance even when the Umayyads built their imperial cities outside the town. Cordova itself, unlike the palace cities of al-Zahra' and al-Zahira, did not vanish when the Umayyad Caliphate came to an end and the city ceased to be the capital of al-Andalus. Like Kairouan, however, it diminished greatly in size, becoming a small country town in which the monuments of its grandeur have not been swamped by the enterprise of a later age.

All ended happily:

> *May clouds like udders stream on palace towers,*
> *   on parks and glades their milk of kindness rain;*
> *For when my arrows all had missed the mark,*
> *   no bounds for me in mountain-top or plain,*
> *God's answer was the circling ocean's swell*
> *   beneath me on the passage into Spain;*
> *Where Cordova embraced me straightaway,*
> *   all dirty with the journey's dusty stain.*[15]

The poet thus came to the point, the hymn of praise, most often to the prince from whom he expected a handsome reward. The utmost skill was called for to address a benefactor who fully appreciated the art of verse.

Like the rising sun, the monarch had transformed the lives of all around. The revelation of his glory was greeted by an opening salute:

> *He came: the thickness of the veil rolled back,*
> *   the wing of darkness turned to rapid flight;*
> *Shrivelled the glimmering meadow of the stars,*
> *   the crack of dawn let in the flood of light.*[16]

In the garden of this splendid day, the fortunate rejoiced. The streams were silver and the flowers gold; the trees were heavy with fruit:

> *Praise that shakes him brings down wealth in showers,*
> *   as fruit is scattered from a shaken tree;*
> *Unblinkingly enjoy his countenance:*
> *   the hands are rain below the sun you see.*[17]

Right: Fourteenth-century wooden panel from North Africa. The bold, deeply carved motifs of arches, pine cones and stems above the Kufic lettering of the inscription are organized around the fans of peacocks' tails which are typical of the Nasrid period in Granada. The fans carry on the tradition of the scallop-shell shape, an image of great antiquity in the Middle East. The shape was widely used in Islam for the head of the mihrab niche, for example, or the corner-pieces beneath a dome of the Fatimid period. The shell was meanwhile adopted as the badge of St James of Compostela, the sign of the Christian conquest.

Idyllic as it might be, this fertility of benefaction was not without effort. The garden was made possible by the sword which kept the enemy at bay. The prince was a warrior, scarlet with the blood of his foes. While the poet solicited the gift of a beautiful girl, he also desired a thoroughbred horse and jewelled weapons to prove his worth in the garden of war. Gems in the hilt were a mark of the sovereign's esteem, but the virtue of a blade was in the steel:

> The sword a stream upon whose double edge
> blood flowers like the red anemone.[18]

A coat of mail was like the rippling of the wind on water, but the comparison was deceptive. The blows of the enemy glanced off the metal fabric, while the wearer's lance plunged into the heart of the fully-armoured opponent like a rope into a well. Above all, the charger made the champion:

> The red roan's torch the tumult takes
> to light the torches of the host at war;
> Triumphant in the pomegranate's hue,
> ears pricked like leaves of myrtle to the fore,
> A bubble from his swirling cup of wine
> leaps laughing to his forehead in a star.[19]

With these accoutrements, and so great a captain, heroism was uncontrolled. To fight was to carouse:

> What, cowardice, with weapons at my side,
> or weakness when decision goes before?
> In you I have a lion strong of claw
> that guards its cubs beneath its drumming roar;
> Sing me the neighing of the steeds, the song I love;
> let gleaming blood fill me the cup of war;
> Set down my saddle on the sun-baked earth, my bed,
> the banners for my tent; I need no more.[20]

Above: Gold necklace of the early fourteenth century from Bentarique, Granada. The filigree beads are of finely worked gold wire. A woman's ornament, the necklace represented personal wealth as well as personal beauty. As a work of art, adding perfection to the perfect, it provided Ibn Hazm with the title of his dissertation on the art of love, 'The Collar of the Dove'.

It was a gallant company that rode to victory beneath the fluttering flags, writing in deeds the lines the poet wrote in words:

> For God the knights have let their pennants fly
> as hawks upon your highness' foemen bent;
> Their spears shall dot the i's their swords inscribe,
> dust dry the ink, and blood the paper scent.[21]

As swordsmanship and penmanship combine in this characteristic image, the author is beginning to take leave of his subject and his work. Rendered permanent and precious by calligraphy, the action he describes will become an object fit for presentation. When the sand has blotted the pages, the lingering odour will be not blood but the fragrance of the perfume sprinkled on the manuscript. Only the dead remain to mention:

> The dead lie numbered with the rocks and stones;
> the vultures rip their bowels, eat the rib-cage bare,
> Bespattered with their feast as if they were
> old women with the henna in their wispy hair.[22]

The prince stands at the summit of his power and fame, like the victorious 'Abd al-Mu'min, caliph of the Almohads, upon the Rock of Gibraltar:

> Ignore the sun, think Saturn's measure short;
> see on the mountain top the peak of peaks.[23]

The poet retires, leaving his masterpiece to the appreciation of the audience, the admiration of the world. Creation is complete when, in the final image, the words themselves become the deed. The monarch's name is incense cast by the author upon the fire of his intellect to fill the universe with its scent.

Poetry after this fashion embraced all these themes and more, from the sublime to the trivial. Its prestige as the mark of the true Arab made it the accomplishment of every educated person from the prince to the student, whether as versifier or connoisseur. Women, in an ostensibly masculine society which was not infrequently dominated by its great ladies, made their contribution.

As a monument to the eloquence of the race, the verse which resulted was carefully preserved. Along with the theologians, jurists and holy men whose lives had been an ornament to the Muslim community, its authors found a place in the immense biographical dictionaries of famous men

Above: Hawking. Detail from a carved ivory inlay of the Fatimid period in Egypt. The saker of English falconry takes its name from the Arabic for a hawk, a bird which united the military aristocracies of Islam and Christian Europe in a common enthusiasm.

which were one of the characteristic products of the civilization. Their works were critically discussed in elegant rhyming prose, couplets in which the second phrase would repeat the sense of the first in so many different words. The enormous vocabulary of Arabic was ransacked to do justice to the theme. Local patriotism is apparent in the twelfth century writer Ibn Bassam, whose *Treasure of the Beauties of the People of the Island* narrated the achievements of the poets of al-Andalus since Arabic was first written in the peninsula, with copious quotations from their *diwans* or collected works, and extensive comparisons of their language and imagery with that of the more famous poets of the east. In *The Pennants of the Champions and the Standards of the Distinguished*, composed by Ibn Sa'id in the thirteenth century, this kind of treatment became simple anthology, with brief extracts from verse written by kings, ministers, doctors of the Law and other men of distinction besides those classified as poets. The strong tendency was to isolate and appreciate individual lines and turns of phrase, stressing the verse which captured an impression in a verbal gem. It was a literature for the exquisite taste of cultured gentlemen in their hours of leisure.

The poet, on the other hand, composed for an immediate audience, not for the public of the future. He offered his poem to that audience, moreover, as a challenge calling for an apt retort. The exchange might be civil, as between friends, or more pointed between lovers. For the recognized poet, bidding for the favour of a royal patron with eulogies to win him a place at court, repartee was a livelihood. Very conscious of their artistic worth, such poets sought to score off each other in the eyes of the world. Famous rivalries developed between them as they matched verse for verse, turning each line back upon its author. When Ibn Sharaf boasted of his noble birth, punning on his name with its meaning of high-born, aristocratic, Ibn Rashiq recalled his own humble birth, which had given him nothing but his genius. Over the many years they spent at the court of Kairouan in the eleventh century, they fought out their running

Above and below: Tilework patterns from the Alcazar of Seville, rebuilt in imitation of the Alhambra by King Pedro the Cruel of Castile, who brought craftsmen from Granada to direct the work in the mid-fourteenth century.

battle of ingenuity, says their biographer, 'like tigers', to the undoubted delight of the sultan whose fame was enhanced by their virtuosity.

Poets like these lent polish to an already polite society. Privately they would accompany the monarch, to make him laugh with the wickedness of their wit at the expense of his entourage, as much as to charm his aesthetic sense with their treatment of whatever subject the occasion offered. As a special favour they might be drawn into the intimate seclusion of the prince's own apartments, and 'invited to share in his many blessings'. Publicly they would speak for him, eulogizing his actions, rebutting the accusations of his enemies, attacking them in return with savage scorn. Politics were polemics, and in the war of words a good poet was greatly to be feared and much desired. Sure of his value, he could pick and choose. Ibn Rashiq refused to go to Spain because, he said, the princelings of Andalus were cats blown up as lions. Ibn Sharaf, who went, preferred the fire of their hospitality. Al-Darimi threw the gift of meat and flour from the ruler of Denia in the face of the messenger who presented it to him as he disembarked, and went on to Valencia until he was lured to the court of Toledo.

The behaviour of the poet was a mirror of the society, his verse the final form of a way of life modelled upon its images. Stylization went very deep in a civilization which had no drama, but acted out its sense of the theatrical in its manner of living. Monarchs were seen to be noble, warriors proud, saints venerable. The plot lay in the fulfilment of these roles, or in their conflict. When the Christian envoys marched out to the palace of al-Zahra' through an endless tunnel of uplifted swords, they expected to find the caliph resplendent on his throne. Instead they found him in rags on the ground, the Koran in front of him. Such contrasts were the delight of a culture which juxtaposed white camphor and black musk, fair-skinned Europeans and dark Ethiopians, lilies and roses, rubies and pearls. The delight was all the greater when the contrast was amusing. Satire, which held its victims up to ridicule, provided the comedy, but a comedy which stood next to tragedy. A man might laugh at his own expense, then kill. The game of mockery, as dangerous as it was attractive, called for nice judgment. It was a difficult moment for the two ministers of the caliph 'Abd al-Rahman III when the sovereign ordered them, each in turn, to satirize the other. Both, unwilling to make a mortal enemy, refused, whereupon their master began:

> Old Abu 'l-Qasim has a long beard,
>   a mile down the length of its tress.

Ibn Jahwar, compelled to carry on, continued:

> Spread to the sides, its width is two miles;
>   mind boggles at such a great truss;
> When he requires to get the thing clean,
>   the Nile is too small for the wash.

To this Abu 'l-Qasim was obliged to reply:

> God's trusted servant finds in his verse
>   my whiskers are long to excess;
> The son of a donkey, hee-hawing away,
>   has brayed like an eater of grass;
> But for my shame before our true guide,
>   my goad I would stick up 'is . . .[24]

The huge mass of the Comares Tower is reflected in the pool of the Court of the Myrtles, the first of the two great inner courts of the Royal Palace of the Alhambra. Built by Yusuf I between 1333 and 1354, the court is a rectangle laid out north and south in keeping with the practice of the period. Here, on the north side, the customary portico frames the entrance to a long hall, the Sala de la Barca, running across the width of the court. The Sala de la Barca, however, which would normally have been the main apartment, is only the antechamber to the great Hall of the Ambassadors, situated inside the massive tower. Nine windows, three in each of the outer walls of the tower, look out over Granada; in the alcove of the central window, seen through the entrance from the court, the monarch had his throne. Inscriptions at the entrance to the Sala de la Barca and to the Hall compare the structure to the bride at her wedding, the new moon lit by the glory of the royal sun.

Light from the Mirador de la Daraja is reflected upon the arches leading out of the Hall of the Two Sisters, las Dos Hermanas. The Hall itself opens off the colonnade around the Court of the Lions. This, the second of the two great courts of the Alhambra, was built by the Sultan Muhammad al-Ghani to celebrate his capture of Algeciras in 1369. Just as the eye travels from the Court of the Myrtles to the far window of the Hall of the Ambassadors, so it travels through the dim interior of las Dos Hermanas to the opening on the world outside. But whereas the windows of the Hall of the Ambassadors look out above Granada, those of the little Mirador look out upon the garden of the Daraja, the most probable site of the private apartments, the harem or 'forbidden area' destroyed in the sixteenth century.

'Ass', said the caliph, supplying the rhyme. 'My lord,' observed Abu 'l-Qasim, 'now you are the satirist, not I.' Very neatly, he was quits with his fellow minister, while the odium rested with the ruler, who was beyond reproach. 'Abd al-Rahman laughed, and rewarded him.

Su cul, ''is ass''; the little vulgarity is as nothing compared to the obscenities of full-blooded derision to be found elsewhere in the literature. What is important is that it is in Spanish, not Arabic. It recalls the existence of two other forms of poetry, peculiar to Andalus, the *muwashshah* and the *zajal*, which, although they are in Arabic, are broken into stanzas with complicated rhyming patterns, and introduce whole lines in the Romance language of the peninsula. As in this anecdote, the subject-matter and its treatment are well below the highest flights of the classical verse, elaborating the bawdy and erotic streak in Arabic poetry for the pleasure of a public as far away as Baghdad. More significant is the reminder that Muslim Spain was bilingual. Against the background of the Spanish vernacular, and of the Arabic dialect which served in the same way as a language of everyday speech, to be Arab in high literary culture was to belong to a nobility of achievement, of personal merit. The secretary, the man who composed and wrote the letters, deeds and charters of the state in flowing script and elevated diction, was an aristocrat. But the man who was Arab by birth was a member of the true élite.

The proof was in the pedigree. 'Abd al-Rahman ibn Muhammad ibn 'Abd Allah ibn Muhammad ibn 'Abd al-Rahman ibn al-Hakam ibn Hisham ibn 'Abd al-Rahman ibn Mu'awiya ibn Hisham ibn 'Abd al-Malik ibn Marwan ibn al-Hakam ibn Abi 'l-'As ibn Umayya . . .: few could compare with the lineage of the great caliph. In the whole of the Maghrib only the Idrisids of Fes, descendants of the Prophet himself, might claim superiority. Genealogies were nevertheless carefully preserved and cultivated by anyone with any pretentions, pushed further and further back until they blended into the lineages of the Arab tribes in the days before Islam. Many were dubious. Their strength lay in the title they conferred upon their owner.

The title in question had a different function from the title of the beduin to membership of the lineage groups which wandered and fought over hundreds of miles of desert and mountain. In the society of the cities it was a claim to consideration and prestige. Collectively it was racial, a title to rule which in the eighth century the Arab armies had ruthlessly asserted. This it remained, even as the definition of an Arab broadened into the cultural with the argument that Arab blood gave rise to Arab genius, and the products of Arab genius were the result of Arab blood:

> The capital city of Cordova, since the island of Andalus was conquered, has been the highest of the high, the furthest of the far, the place of the standard, the mother of towns; the abode of the good and godly, the homeland of wisdom, its beginning and its end; the heart of the land, the fount of science, the dome of Islam, the seat of the imam; the home of right reasoning, the garden of the fruits of ideas, the sea of the pearls of talent. From its horizon have arisen the stars of the earth and the banners of the age, the cavaliers of poetry and prose. Out of it have come pure compositions and exquisite compilations. And the reason for this, and for the distinction of its people before and since, as compared with others, is that the horizon encompasses none but the seekers and the searchers after all the various kinds of knowledge and refinement. Most of the people of the country are noble Arabs from the east who conquered it, lords of the troops of Syria and Iraq who settled there, so that their descendants remain in each district as a noble race. Hardly a town lacks a skilled writer, a compelling poet, who had he praised it, the least would have been great.[25]

Bound together in this way, the criteria of race and culture worked on the society of the Maghrib in paradoxical fashion. The reciprocity of life and literary art created images of superiority and inferiority which refined the broad classifications of mankind in the Muslim social order, and gave expression to the uneasy relationships within the Muslim community itself. The Arab nomads who spread across North Africa from the eleventh century onwards, and made their appearance in Andalus in the Moroccan armies, were not welcomed or even recognized as brothers from the distant past, endowed with the virtue of old. They were disliked and feared as dangerous aliens whose low brown tents threatened to engulf the towns and villages of a settled land. Barely Muslim, living by unwritten custom instead of by the written Law, the language they spoke was not the language of the Koran and the classical odes but a barbarous vernacular far below the level of literacy. The

After the sack of Cordova and the end of the Umayyad Caliphate, the ivory carvers of the old capital took refuge at Cuenca in the dominions of the Little Kings of Toledo. The casket, of which this is the end panel, is of wood covered with gilded leather and openwork ivory plaques showing scenes from a fanciful hunt. The inscription gives the name and the pedigree of the heir to the throne, for whom it was made in 1049–50. It fell into Christian hands presumably when the city was captured in 1085. It was probably at the monastery of Silos that the corners in cloisonné enamel were added in the twelfth century.

repulsion they induced was only exceeded by the legendary horror of the Berbers, dating in all probability from the insurrections of the eighth century, and perpetuated in North Africa and Spain by their existence as rough mountaineers, speaking an incomprehensible tongue, and liable to serve as uncouth soldiers for the repression of the civilian population. In the legend of Andalus before Islam, the fear is explained and justified.

According to the legend, Andalus was first settled by Greeks fleeing from the Persians. By their wisdom and diligence, they transformed the country into the most fertile land on earth, so fertile that they grew afraid of invasion. Only two nations were dangerous, the Arabs and the Berbers, the lords of famine and want. The Arabs at that time were far away, but the Berbers came closer, until only the Straits separated them from the Island. So, while one of the kings of Andalus built an aqueduct across the sea from Africa to bring water to turn the mills, another constructed a talisman, a gigantic statue of a Berber with beard and lock of frizzy hair, sandals, and a cloth wrapped round the body, the two ends held in the left hand. In the outstretched right hand was a key which would fall whenever a Berber ship came in sight. Both the statue and the aqueduct (whose remains can be seen in the Rock of Gibraltar) may have been imagined from the relics of Rome. Like the story of King Roderic and the casket, however, the legend had a contemporary purpose; it may well have taken on a new lease of life with the coming of the Almoravids and the Almohads.

The Prophet himself, it was said, had warned his followers against the Berbers, the worst race on earth. In reply, the Berbers quoted Muhammad's words of praise for a people excellent in Islam, whose piety far exceeded that of the materially-minded Arabs. In the long run, however, they were unable to hold out against the strength of the Arab case. The Berbers were alleged to be the offspring of Jalut (Goliath) from the land of the Philistines. The opinion gained ground that they were, in fact, Arabs who had emigrated from the land of Himyar in the Yemen in the days before Islam. Himyar had once been green and prosperous, irrigated by the waters of the great dam of Ma'rib on the edge of the Empty Quarter of Arabia. But the dam had burst, and the waters had destroyed what they had once brought to life. The king and his people had left to wander the earth. That they had arrived in the Maghrib was a happy thought. When the Berber sultan Mu'izz ibn Badis repudiated his allegiance to the Fatimids in the eleventh century, he claimed descent from the old lords of the Yemen, an ancestry far older than that of the masters of Cairo. When he abandoned Kairouan, it was abandoned like Ma'rib, inundated not by water but a flood of beduin. As Himyarites, its people fled as far as Spain.

As Himyarites, more significantly, the Almoravids conquered the country. The men of Andalus might be dismayed by Yusuf ibn Tashfin, who spoke hardly any Arabic, and dismissed their poets as fancy beggars. His son 'Ali, however, was a protagonist of Arab ancestry as well as Arab faith. No more was heard of any satire of the race by those who, in perfect Arabic, were pleased to boast of their non-Arab descent, be it Berber or Spanish. The aggressive Arabism of the Almoravids survived their fall. Although the Almohads were Berbers who specifically rejected the claim of the Veiled Men to be Arabs, by the second half of the twelfth century the Christian threat from the north was unmistakable. Not to be Arab was not to be a patriot. The argument was clinched by holy war.

In the Court of the Lions in the Alhambra the fountain's inscription proclaims the glory of the ruler who feeds the lions of holy war as water feeds the lions of the fountain.

THE PICTURE OF THE WORLD

The peacocks of the Cope of King Robert surround themselves with their tails. They adorn a robe, the greater part of which is preserved in the Church of St Sernin at Toulouse, a principal stage upon the pilgrims' road to Santiago de Compostela. Its name seems quite arbitrary; the earliest mention of the semicircular silk cloth describes it as a chasuble employed to wrap the relics of St Exupéry in 1258. 'King Robert' would have been Robert of Anjou, King of Naples, 1309–43. The fabric is Andalusian, of the twelfth–thirteenth century. The motif is the traditional one of symmetrical figures which confront each other on either side of a central tree, extending to the minor figures of the antelopes and smaller birds, and to the inscription above and below, Al-Baraka al-Kamila, 'Perfect Blessing', which is written both right to left and left to right. But the circular borders which would once have surrounded the figures and contained the inscription have disappeared, leaving only the illusion created by the peacocks' tails. Instead, the motif is arranged in bands in the manner of the later period, a pattern accentuated by the colours. Rows of birds in red alternate with rows of birds in yellow on the blue ground.

When the world was once again inhabited after the Flood, the inhabited area was in the shape of a bird whose head was in the east, its wings to the north and south, its body in the middle and its tail in the west. Because of this identification with the vilest part of the creature, the west was despised until the time when the Greeks settled in Spain. Then by their diligence Andalus became so fair that those who saw it said: The bird in whose likeness the inhabited world was formed was no ordinary bird, but a peacock whose beauty is in the tail.

The story has the familiar appearance of a legend devised to explain a fact with all the delight in imagery and paradox which fills the poetry of the Arabs. An intense and sumptuous vision of splendour arises from the narrative, standing for the truth which the words proclaim. Contained within this vision are the elements of a visual as well as a literary art. The narrative which explains, the symbol which represents, and the form which decorates, are familiar from the European Middle Ages, in which the stories of the Old and New Testament, for example, generate the images which adorn the walls of the great cathedrals in mosaic, paint, glass and stone. Art of this kind did not appear on the same scale in Islam. The reason is not simply an aversion to the sacred image, the substitution of a sacred script. It is to be found more generally in the gorgeous spreading of the peacock's tail. In the art of Islam, the pictorial image was gradually subordinated to the decorative effect.

Figures became shapes to fill a space which was often circular, upon a surface which was frequently curved. Their outlines turned and twisted in an overall design. Surrounded by foliage, they receded into patterns of leaves and branches. The letters of the script became the knotted roots of stems and fronds. Representation and writing ran together in a maze of boughs, shoots and tendrils. The elaborate combinations of stylized forms resolved themselves into intricate networks of abstract lines, sinuous and straight. Thus discarded, figurative art in the Maghrib did not revive under the influence of the illuminated manuscripts of Iran, Syria and Egypt. The taste of Christian Spain reintroduced the pictorial element into the art of the Mudejars, and eventually into the decoration of the Alhambra. But in the face of those who dared to portray the likeness of God Himself, the geometry of the arabesque itself became a symbol of the faith, endlessly repeated across every facet of the Muslim world.

The image represented by the story of the peacock was not thereby lost. The defiant glorification of Andalus to the rest of Islam depended upon a fundamental perception, the perception of a civilized zone

stretching over the known earth from the circling ocean in the west to the circling ocean in the east, between the extremes of heat and cold to south and north. It was a perception which came naturally to the adherents of a religion which had spread out along a zone of this kind, and who from its western extremity looked backwards to the east with a certain feeling of provincial inferiority, but to the north and south with nothing except a sense of superiority to barbarous infidels. Their mental geography thrived on the experience of travel, trade and war, which familiarized the men of the Maghrib with the east as a source of instruction, and with Christian Europe and black Africa as a source of slaves. It was elaborated in the accounts of travellers who wrote of their journeys, and in the compilations of those who collected the information provided by others.

The first descriptions are from the east. The *Surat al-Ard* or 'Picture of the Earth' by Ibn Hawqal shows the Spain of 'Abd al-Rahman III through the eyes of a visitor who compares its cities and its products with those of Iraq. The unruly Galicians, the Basques, the Franks and 'the Slavs' who stretch beyond them into the steppes of Asia, provide the slaves, especially the eunuchs, who are exported as far as the borders of India. The gold trade across the western Sahara is conducted with cheques of a value unheard-of in Iran. Not until a hundred years later do we find in the *Routes and Kingdoms* of al-Bakri the view of a man of the west, fascinated by the place-names of ancient Arabia to the point of listing them in a dictionary for readers of the classical literature, and in his wider geography a mine of information from the more recent past.

Legend, which distorts both time and space, identifies Tunisia with Macedon, the home of Alexander the Great, locates the spot where Moses parted from Elijah, and tells of a perpetually bleeding corpse in a cave in the mountains of Algeria. It does not, however, interfere with the plotting of routes and the factual description of recognizable places in a recognizable landscape. This landscape extends far to the south across the Sahara, where the caravans may go for as much as eight days without finding water, to the kingdom of Ghana in the land of the blacks from

Left and below: Under the Norman Kings, pressures upon the large Muslim population of Sicily gradually increased. Oppression culminated in a cycle of revolt and repression which ended in the thirteenth century, when those Muslims who remained were deported to the Italian mainland. Meanwhile their craftsmen produced, often for Christian patrons, ivories like this box and this comb, in which the decoration is painted, not carved, upon the surface. The box is of wood, plated with ivory; the figure of the musician with the chubby face shows Fatimid influence, although the arabesques on the comb look European. Refugees took the craft to Granada, where it survived.

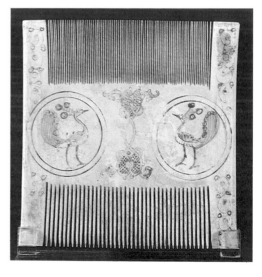

Opposite: A double door within a double door. Each leaf of the great doors, which close the entrances to the halls that open off the Court of the Maidens in the Alcazar of Seville, was provided with a wicket-door to give access when the doors themselves were closed. The huge leaf, here folded back against the wall, turned on posts in the pavement below and in a bracket above. The shadow of the deeply-lobed arch of the portico falls across the pattern formed by the complicated joints.

which eyewitnesses have returned to describe a gilded majesty in the midst of the African bush. How far it extended to the north we do not know, for only a part of al–Bakri's great work survives. But in the twelfth century, at the court of King Roger II in Palermo, the Moroccan al–Idrisi wrote his *Book of Roger*, in which he described Europe as far as Scandinavia.

Within two hundred years after the last of the pagan Norsemen had ravaged the Atlantic coasts of the Maghrib, therefore, their homeland was known in some detail. Ireland was the headquarters of the pirates. Denmark was flat and sandy, Norway a vast empty island or peninsula with the tallest trees in the world. It was the land of the beaver, where the crops never ripened, but were cut when green, and subsequently dried. England, Normandy, a small kingdom of France around Paris on its

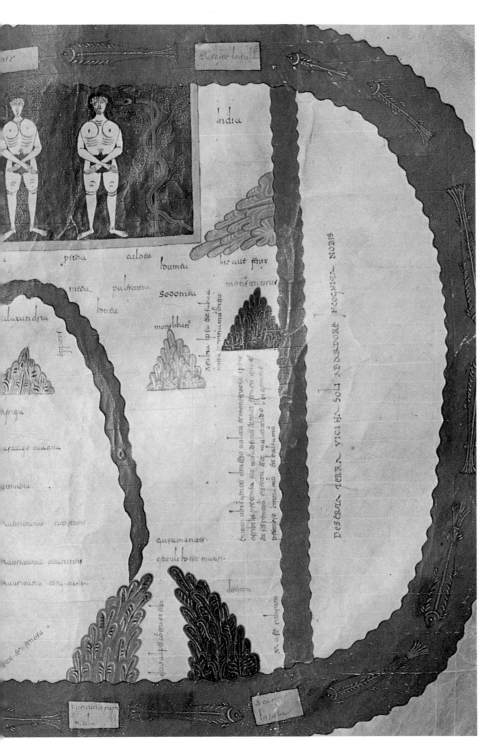

Mental rather than physical geography; a Mozarabic map of the world, designed to illustrate the preaching of the Apostles. It is a schematic and highly traditional representation; although it was made in the middle of the eleventh century, its sole concession to modernity is the horseshoe arch of the city of Jerusalem, which even so hardly differs from its Visigothic prototype. No special place is allotted to Santiago de Compostela, the shrine of the Apostle James who was the patron saint of the northern Christians. The names are in fact all Roman: North Africa for example is divided into the old Roman provinces, Africa, Numidia and the three Mauretanias. Places such as Cordova and Kairouan do not exist. West is at the bottom of the map, with the Mediterranean upright in the middle; Spain is therefore the wedge-shape on the left, closed off by the pink triangle of the Pyrenees. At the head of the Mediterranean the blue 'Y' which extends to the circling ocean is the Black Sea fed by the Danube; Constantinople is at the fork. In the other direction the Nile curves down to the west; further to the right is the red line of the Red Sea, beyond which, in the far south, is desert 'unknown to us'. At the top of the map in the east, Adam and Eve stand in the earthly Paradise, flanked by the Caucasus on the left and India on the right. Jerusalem stands at the centre of the world; around the edge is the river of ocean. Britain and Ireland appear as yellow oblongs, bottom left. The naïvety of the diagram, however, clearly brings out the concept of a world originating in the east, where the garden of heaven is situated, and focussed upon a holy city in the middle. It was this concept which underlay the Muslim picture of the earth, slowly transformed into a realistic map by the steady accumulation of information about the surface of a terrestrial globe.

island in the Seine; Burgundy, Flanders and Saxony; Austria, Bohemia, Hungary; Poland, Estonia, Latvia, Finland and Russia; all these and more took the place of the vast undifferentiated territory of 'the Franks and the Slavs' perceived by Ibn Hawqal.

The quantity of information was a direct result of the rapid growth of Christian Europe in the interval. One of the more spectacular signs of this growth, the arrival of the Normans in Sicily, helped supply the intelligence. To the east, the continued expansion of the Muslim world – creating sultanates in India and establishing colonies of merchants in China – brought to the men of the west personal experience of what they had previously only read about in books. In the fourteenth century Ibn Battuta converted a pilgrimage to Mecca into twenty-four years of travel to the Far East. When he was in the imperial capital of China he encountered a man from Ceuta, a city a few miles from his home city of Tangier, who was now a prosperous physician to a foreign people. Miraculously, as he prepared on his return to North Africa to cross the Sahara, Ibn Battuta met the man's brother at Sijilmasa on the edge of the desert. His travels continued from here down into the western Sudan, where he presented himself in true Andalusian fashion to the emperor of Mali, saying: 'I have travelled through the countries of the world and met their kings. Here have I been four months in your country, yet you have neither shown me hospitality nor given me anything. What am I to say of you before other rulers?' Gratified with gold from this, the land of gold, he describes a monarch dressed in red European velvet, the Muslim master of a tropical world on the cultural horizon of the Mediterranean.

The arts of Arabic composition do not by themselves explain this substantial geographical literature, however much it may dwell upon the world of Islam, and upon the association of places with the notable events and the notable people that filled its history. In China Ibn Battuta admired the porcelain which the Arabs and Persians had tried hard to imitate; he was enormously impressed by the portraiture which produced such perfect likenesses of all foreigners that if any one committed an offence and fled, his picture could be circulated. The fabled wisdom which had come to rest in the hands of the Chinese, however, had descended into the brains of the Greeks, and it was the Greek sciences which provided the spatial dimensions for Arab conceptions. The Muslim might declare such knowledge superfluous if not erroneous, superseded by revelation; the Arab might affect to despise it as ignoble. In fact, the measurement of the earth proceeded with the help of the 'Arabic' numerals which came from India in the eighth century, on the basis of the geography of the Greek writer Ptolemy.

Star-shaped 'tile' of stucco or carved plaster, the centre of a knot of lines which radiated outwards until they interlocked with those from other octangles in a regular pattern extending to infinity. In the shield-shapes which formed at the intersections, Mudejar craftsmen inserted the arms of their Christian lords, a practice adopted by the Nasrids of Granada. Painted and gilded, the central stars carried their own motifs. In this example of the thirteenth or fourteenth century, probably from Toledo, an inscription forms the emblem. Distorted almost out of recognition, the letters of the foliated Kufic script intertwine to produce the lobed arch which is the principal feature of the device.

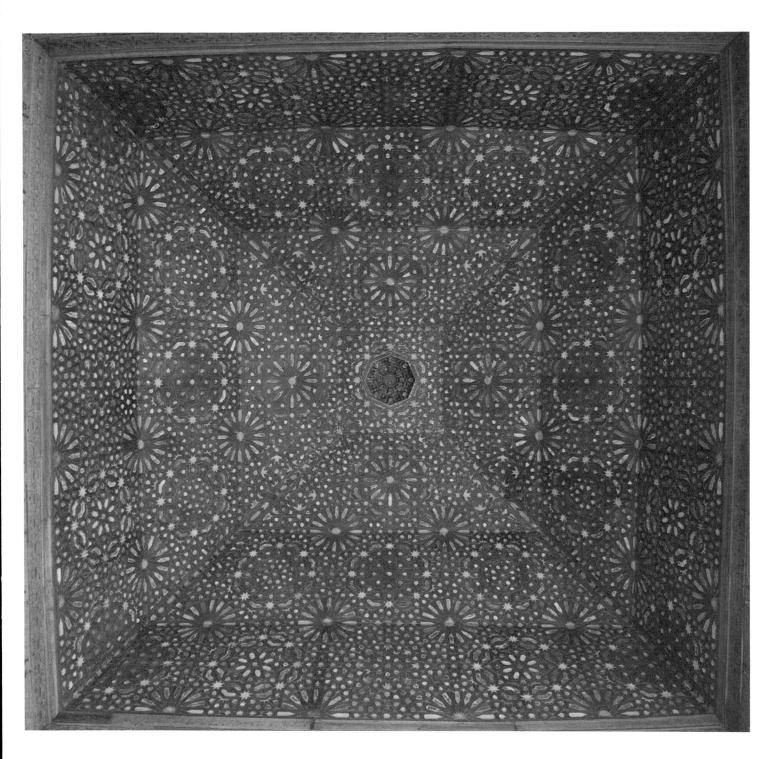

The circumference of the round earth was calculated with reasonable accuracy, and its surface divided into degrees of latitude and longitude. Latitude gave precision to the notion of zones, and a scheme to writers like Idrisi, who divides the world into seven climates from south to north, each in ten sections from west to east. The description proceeds methodically, running from section to section along each climate in turn. If the result is confusing, with a great deal of overlap and consequent repetition between sections and between climates, that is because the immense task of mapping the globe in accordance with these principles had scarcely begun.

Idrisi did provide his reader with maps to make clear, for example, the bewildering information that part of England was in the north-west corner of the second section of the sixth climate; it was fortunate that Andalus fitted nicely into the first section of the fourth. But apart from

The roof of the sky. The domed wooden ceiling of the Hall of the Ambassadors in the Royal Palace of the Alhambra employs the star-shaped patterns of geometrical interlace to represent the seven heavens with six rows of stars crowned by a cupola. By the blessing of God, the master of the universe, the sun is the king who sits enthroned in the alcove of the window below, looking inwards upon his exquisite domain.

the uncertainty of the true direction or distance of one place from another, the projection was elementary. King Roger had made a huge disc of silver, 450 pounds (200 kilograms) in weight, upon which the continents were engraved with rigorous attention to the master drawing, complete with every detail. To this planisphere the *Book of Roger* supplied the commentary, and from it, or from some comparable representation, were taken the sectional maps for each copy of the volume. The world thus depicted was certainly round but essentially flat and wholly disproportionate. Contained with the encircling ocean along the rim, Asia was grotesquely shrunk and Africa enlarged to fill the southern hemisphere. The effects of globular form were not envisaged.

By contrast, the heavens were rendered spherically in practice as well as in theory. When Idrisi first came to Palermo, it is said, he was provided with almost ten times as much silver to make a model of the cosmos. He did so by a series of silver hoops one inside the other. Since these used only a little of the metal, he kept the remainder as a gift, with much else added by a grateful king. If the story is true, the model may have been an early example of the armillary sphere, that is, a sphere made up of three rings to represent the apparent motion of the heavenly bodies round the earth. One, the meridian, was a great circle of longitude passing through the celestial poles about which the sky revolves. The second was the celestial equator, a great circle of latitude corresponding to the equator of the earth. The third, the ecliptic, was the great circle in which the sun moves through the year against the background of the fixed stars, from sign to sign of the Zodiac. Hinged together with other rings of the same kind, they would make an instrument which could be used to calculate positions on the earth and in the sky.

Normally, however, such calculations would be made with the astrolabe, a metal disc hanging vertically from a ring. Right across one face, pivoted in the middle like the needle of a compass, was a pointer equipped with sights to measure the elevation of a star above the horizon against a scale around the rim. The reading thus obtained could then be used to set the dial on the other side of the disc. There, the hoops of the armillary sphere were compressed into a two-dimensional grid of circles and semicircles cut from a single plate, turning above a sky map engraved on the disc itself to a stereographic projection of the kind now used for polar maps. This showed the heavens centred on the Pole Star, as far south as the Tropic of Capricorn. At the same time lines of latitude and longitude, almucantars and azimuths, were marked about the zenith, the point directly over the observer's head, to indicate the visible area.

Since the zenith varied according to the position of the observer on the surface of the earth, it was necessary to have a different astrolabe for each terrestrial latitude. To meet this difficulty Ibn al-Zarqali, known to the Latin West as Arzachel, employed a horizontal instead of a vertical polar projection. The grid of the traditional astrolabe, turning above the representation of the heavens, was furnished with spikes to indicate the major stars. When the grid was turned to bring the star selected to its apparent height, the position of all the rest would be shown, as well as that of the sun in the Zodiac. A pointer like the hand of a clock revolving round the Pole Star in the centre of the dial would, when turned to the position of the sun, give its direction and the precise time of the year from figures round the edge. In this way the pious Muslim could ascertain the way to face for prayer, while the astrologer could acquire the information for a horoscope. Both were indebted to the accumulated knowledge which made the instrument possible to construct. In return, their observations and their calculations refined that knowledge to the

The Caird Astrolabe, most probably made in France about 1300 to a Moorish design. The Latin letters transcribe the Arabic names of the stars; Arabic figures are (wrongly) used for 4, 5 and 7. On the back of the instrument, on the left, the alidade or pointer turns to measure the altitude of the stars. On the face, the grid of the rete or 'net' is equipped with 28 spikes pointing to the position of the named stars on the map of the heavens engraved on the plate below. South is at the top, below the ring. The map is valid only for a given latitude; this astrolabe is therefore equipped with seven such maps on seven interchangeable plates, ranging from 15° to 48.8°, which is marked for Paris, Chartres and Sens.

exactness of the elaborate tables of the planetary movements compiled by Arzachel, his predecessors and his successors.

Such men, for the majority, were wizards, and their science was a mystery. In the folklore of North Africa, which has survived down to the twentieth century, the earth is flat, with mountains like pegs or weights to hold it down. Below it is a subterranean world of darkness in which the first man and woman wandered until the ant led them out through its hole to teach them to grow crops and keep animals. The sky lay close to the ground until a woman hit her head on it and told it to go away. Cosmic events are plotted on home ground: the Djurdjura mountains of Algeria were the home of the first bull. Islam has reinforced this habit of identification: Adam and Eve were created out of earth from the Doukkala region of Morocco. Nevertheless there are traces of explanations of a different order. An elementary confusion of physical light with spiritual enlightenment appears in the belief that the world remained in darkness from the time of its creation to the birth of the Prophet. When Muhammad was born the sun began to shine, the moon appeared, and it was spring. More elaborate is the concept of seven earths, one on top of the other, each of them a kingdom, of men, of ants, of snakes, of winds, and so on. With the seven earths go seven seas, and over all are seven heavens, of ice, of iron, of copper, of silver, of gold, of rubies, and finally of light, each with its own inhabitants. Intruding into the list of plants with medicinal or magical properties to kill or cure is a *rabi'at al-kimiya*, 'alchemical grass', which would, if it were found, open locks and change base metals into gold.

Such explanations stem ultimately from the Greeks, from whom the Arabs received a philosophy they could neither ignore nor wholly assimilate to their faith. The philosophy dealt with the nature of the universe; the problem for the faithful was the explanation it required of the nature of God. The Almoravids, who interpreted literally those scriptural passages which spoke of God's face and hand, without asking how the lord of the worlds could have the features of a man, were denounced as crude anthropomorphists. Those who spoke more plausibly of God's power, will, knowledge and love, on the other hand, encountered other difficulties, since all these qualities attributed to Him seemed to make plural and finite what was single and infinite. They appeared, in other words, to bring God down from the unique height at which He existed, free from all the limitations of space and time, to the level of the mortal world in which everything, even mind, was divided into separate compartments. The problem might seem to be simply a question of language in which words are merely signs. If, however, words had no real meaning, comprehension was totally baffled. On the basis of Greek philosophy, faith sought understanding.

The Greek philosophy inherited by the Arabs was a philosophy of qualities as opposed to quantities, whether it was the quality of a species, the horsiness of a horse, for example, or the quality of a characteristic shared by species, such as the swiftness of a camel and a horse. The syllogism, the form in which its arguments were cast, was a way of comparing and contrasting the possession of these qualities with a view to discovering what more could logically be said about their occurrence. The trivial: All philosophers are wise; Plato and Aristotle are philosophers; therefore Plato and Aristotle are wise, when systematically developed spelt out the rules of being. These rules were the common denominator of the universe; the reasoning behind them was shared by God the creator and man the witness.

This splendid vision of a natural law which informed the world by divine command was apparently opposed to the concept of a revealed Law; the first could be comprehended, the second had to be obeyed. When Ibn Tumart, the Mahdi of the Almohads, arrived in the Maghrib to challenge the Almoravids, he came armed with a theology which employed logic to demonstrate that natural law could not exist. If God, by definition, were omnipotent, then everything was made by Him, including continuity. Nothing could endure a moment unless He wished. He was therefore involved in an act of continuous creation, second by second, of which the result was a set of individual objects. None of the apparent qualities of these objects had any power to make them what they were, since these qualities could at any time be altered by the divinity which ruled as it pleased. A stone was not unchangeably stony. Quicker than the metaphor which could turn flowers into stars and stars into flowers, a miracle could, and on the Day of Judgment would, transform the garden of the world. The natural law of the philosophers, by which stones were the result of stoniness, was simply a description of what God was normally pleased to do. The stoniness of a stone was no more than a reliable coincidence, rather like the magnanimity of sultans, which enabled the poet as a rule to count upon a reward.

A hundred years before Ibn Tumart, the Andalusian Ibn Hazm, more famous for his discourse on the art of love, disagreed. The doctrine of continuous creation sharply distinguished God from man, whose only contribution to the act was a moral intention which made what he did into his spiritual property, good or bad. But as a conscious being, it could be argued that he did in fact resemble his Creator, sharing however imperfectly in the qualities expressed by The Most Beautiful Names, the Living, the Mighty, the Wise, the Hearer, the Seer, the Compassionate,

The gardens of Marrakesh by the long walls of the city, first laid out under the Almohads in the twelfth century. The rectangular pool, divided into four by paths that cross in the middle, displays the fondness for still water only matched by the delight in fountains and in streams. Poetry combined the two pleasures in the image of the wind upon the surface, giving the brief illusion of a page of writing or a coat of chain mail. The evergreen was required to sustain the impression of a paradise in which life never failed. Like the pool, the garden itself was ideally a rectangle, centred upon an isolated pavilion. From there the eye could follow the lines of the composition, past the flowers, shrubs and fruit trees, the roses and the climbing vines, out to a wider horizon. At Marrakesh the snows of the High Atlas close a view which from the walls extends over the palm groves of the city.

the Merciful, the Generous, the Just and many more, which described the attributes of the Holy King. And if man possessed other qualities of evil which could not be attributed to God, that was only because the deity was too good to behave in such ways, and did not choose to do so. This line of thought was taken by Ibn Bajja, a contemporary of the great Unitarian Ibn Tumart, to a point at which the critical distinction between the divine power to make and the human inability to do more than look on trembled on the verge of disappearance.

Ibn Bajja, Latinized as Avempace, was a polymáth, learned in philosophy, astronomy, music, mathematics and medicine, who derived his argument from the hierarchy of the heavens. The seven skies of Moroccan myth were those of Aristotle, the celestial spheres which encased the earth in globe after globe of ethereal fineness, carrying the heavenly bodies in their revolution round the terrestrial core. The lack of an apparent reason for their whirling in one direction rather than another about the static centre from which they were observed by men was a principal argument for the theory of continuous creation. More important for the opponents of that theory was the ascending order of the spheres expressed in the myth by the increasing preciousness of the heavens, from ice and iron up to rubies and to light itself. The imagery of the Arabian Nights, the passage of the hero from cave to cave of ever greater riches in search of the ultimate treasure, gives the association of this rising scale with the journey of the soul to God.

For Ibn Bajja, that journey was the return of mind from matter. The heavens had been the stages of its descent from the immaterial wholeness of pure intellect into the innumerable bodily shapes of earth. At the lowest sphere, that of the moon, eternal thoughtfulness, contemplating only itself, had become creative. An active intelligence had come into existence, conceiving the ways in which to mould the stuff of the world into innumerable forms. From that conception came the world itself, mind passing into matter as the multifarious shapes of the objects which compose it. Concrete expressions of the divine thought, these shapes with all their qualities gave to each object its individual reason, its own particular nature which was the purpose of its being. With mind thus embedded in the things of the world, it was left to man, the highest of these created beings, to reflect upon his surroundings and understand how they were made. His nature and hence his purpose was to be conscious, not only of what he could see and hear and feel, but of the logical principles which governed such physical objects. He enjoyed, in fact, the gift of the speculative mind which, although fragmented and scattered in the crania of the individuals who composed the human race, could aspire by the exercise of reason to comprehend the whole, to attain to the level of the single active intelligence from which it had sprung, and eventually to pass back into the realm of pure intelligibles, the ultimate reality. When that happened, the purpose of creation itself was fulfilled, as the divine intellect regarded itself in the mirror of the world it had made.

In the second half of the twelfth century Ibn Bajja was succeeded by a great man of the world. Ibn Tufayl (Abentofal) was secretary and physician to 'Abd al-Mu'min, the caliph of the Almohads, and physician and chief minister to his son and successor Abu Ya'qub at the Almohad court of Seville. In his most famous work, he clad this intellectual vision in romance. *Hayy ibn Yaqzan*, 'Life, Son of the Wakeful', was the life story of its hero, depicted as cast away in infancy on a desert island to be nursed by a gazelle. By the age of seven the child had learnt by imitation of the animal to take care of itself and express itself in its own way. At fourteen, the death of the animal mother had taught the boy the existence

of something that made the body alive; the discovery of fire had pointed to heaven as the source of this life. By the age of twenty-one the young man was master of his environment. At the same time he had inferred from the multiplicity of shapes and the variety of transformations in the world about him the existence of an external unifying force. By the age of twenty-eight this inference was demonstrable by the movement of the heavens, which pointed to a spherical, finite earth all of whose parts were nevertheless bound together in a single whole. By the age of thirty-five the conclusion was clear, the necessity of an entirely immaterial, utterly perfect creator.

The sting of this philosophy was in the tail. In the second half of his life the natural philosopher, who has attained by reason to the truths of religion, encounters his first fellow human being, a visitor from another island who has come in search of solitude to contemplate the ultimate reality. The visitor finds to his astonishment that what he has learnt from religion as a member of society, Hayy has learnt by himself in purer form. Together they go back to the visitor's home to show Hayy what human society is like. It is discovered to be a matter of sordid interests, its religion a question of rewards and punishments. Only Hayy's companion can see the revelation as a guiding symbol of something beyond; only Hayy, untainted with any normal upbringing, can fully appreciate what that something is. Together they return to the original island to be alone with a knowledge denied to the mass of mankind.

When the Emperor Frederick II, the successor to the Norman kings of Sicily and a similar patron of Arabic science, ordered a child to be brought up without ever being spoken to, to see what language it would speak, the infant died. Ibn Tufayl's little fiction is a monument to a principle rather than a person. Certainly its conclusions were not those of Islam. The reconciliation of reasoning with faith, and of faith with the notion of natural law, was the work of the man whom Ibn Tufayl

Above: Ceramic tile of the fourteenth century, probably from the Alhambra. The blue and lustre paint has lent itself to a splendidly bold and rhythmic arabesque of stems, leaves and birds which seems to anticipate the style of the Renaissance in Europe and of the Ottoman Empire in Islam. Enclosed within the foliage are the arms of the Nasrid sultans, in imitation of their Christian neighbours.

introduced to the caliph, and who succeeded him as imperial physician, Ibn Rushd (Latinized as Averroes). Ibn Rushd was a native of Cordova, of a family learned in the Holy Law, himself on two occasions a qadi. His achievement, however, was the commentaries he wrote on the works of Aristotle, using the traditional scholarly method of explaining the meaning of a text to establish the answers to a range of philosophical questions on a scale to match the expositions of the Shari'a. Advocates of continuous creation were dismissed in his *Destruction of Destruction*. The world and its workings were necessary and invariable because God Himself, by definition, had to be and did not change. Informed by the active intelligence of the deity, they could scarcely be otherwise. The fantastic flight of the mind into a realm of ultimate, immaterial reality was thereby arrested. A world which had to be could not be at the bottom of the scale of being. The qualities which were the laws of its nature were realized in the physical objects they formed from the matter of the elements. Seen by the eye as fleeting individual shapes, perceived by the intellect as permanent generalizations, they remained locked into these things as the stamp of the die in the metal was locked in an Almohad coin. Here lay knowledge, for the mind, being itself a necessary part of the natural order, could be absolutely sure that its logic was that of creation, and that it could in consequence learn the final truth. The disclosures of revelation, the highest secrets of God, were susceptible to rational explanation. In a law-abiding universe, that was as much an article of faith as the converse, that rational explanations must be believed.

This formidable argument for a law of nature was a weighty prescription for the natural sciences, a powerful theoretical justification for their assumptions. *The Sage's Step*, an eleventh-century work on alchemy, required the practitioner to know the Greek writers, to study mathematics, to show skill with the hands, to watch carefully, and to reflect on what he found, for Nature never changed, never produced the same result in different ways. Following the regularities of her behaviour, the alchemist was like a doctor who tried to bring into action the natural forces to restore the natural balance in the body of his patient which had been just as naturally upset. Successive generations of alchemists had indeed accumulated a mass of information about chemical operations and chemical changes besides those that went into the manufacture of brass and steel, gold and silver, glass, glazed pottery, pigments and dyes. Without the same freedom to experiment with the causes, the physicians were expert in following the progress of disease, bringing to bear on its treatment an immense knowledge of herbs and drugs. When the Black Death came to the Kingdom of Granada in 1348–9, its contagious character was perceived, and the infection of the port of Almeria was seen to contrast with the immunity of isolated nomads of North Africa. The minister Lisan al-Din ibn al-Khatib, 'Tongue of Religion, Son of the Preacher', like many another vizier of the time a man of medicine as well as a statesman, took the opportunity to declare that whatever the Traditions of the Prophet might say, their remarks about exhalations from Hell could not stand against the evidence of careful observation.

When *The Sage's Step* describes the preparation of mercuric oxide by the quantities involved it is apparent that the old Greek theory of the four elements, fire, earth, air and water, which in varying combinations of hotness and coldness, dryness and wetness were held to account for the material properties of flesh as well as stone, was in itself no obstacle to scientific discovery. What prevented a scientific revolution was partly prohibition. Reverence for the dead would not permit dissection of the

body; reverence for the living, and no doubt fear of a mistake, made operations a last resort. Ignorance caused by reluctance, and reluctance brought on by ignorance, restricted this essential branch of medicine to the great Abu 'l-Qasim (Abulcasis) al-Zahrawi, physician to the caliph Hakam II, whose writings became the essential textbook of surgery for hundreds of years. In the case of alchemy the search for gold led away from the use of the crucible as the means of inquiry. The conviction that all metals were compounds of sulphur and mercury, and that although mercury smelted with sulphur yielded nothing but a black stone, it should be possible to alter the compound in a base metal to obtain something more precious, called for something more than experiment to effect the transmutation. What was required was the elixir or philosopher's stone. The hymn to its power that circulated in the Arab world had come down, it was said, from remote antiquity, cryptically inscribed upon the emerald tablet held in the hands of the corpse of Hermes Trismegistus (Three Times the Greatest, Thoth, the builder of the Pyramids). The elixir was nothing less than the soul of the universe, reduced to a solid. Once found it would operate as the unity behind diversity, the life that pervaded the human body as well as the stars. The quest to grasp this greatest secret of the world was no longer the concern of the physicist. With Hayy ibn Yaqzan, Ibn Tufayl's fictional hero, a truth was sought of which gold was little more than the symbol. Whatever the satisfactions of the seeking, humanity at large was left with nothing but a tale of 'alchemical grass'.

The plants of the herbalist had magical as well as medicinal properties; the heavens whose movements were so accurately observed and calculated were indicators of fortune. Still more important than these apparent distractions, however, were prevailing social circumstances. The scientist was no narrow specialist. Trained in the mosque schools in the knowledge of Islam, the language and literature of the Arabs, he went

on like Ibn Rushd (Averroes) to embrace the whole wisdom of the Greeks. Professionally he was more limited, obliged to make his living from the skills for which people would pay, above all from astrology and medicine. From the time in the tenth century when the Greek sciences took hold in the Muslim West, the majority of their exponents were either 'men of the stars', doctors, or both. In these capacities they came to court, joining with the poets and the secretaries of state in the service of the monarch, and rising in the case of royal physicians like Ibn Zuhr (Avenzoar), Ibn Tufayl and Ibn Rushd to the rank of vizier. The leaders, in other words, belonged to the circle of statesmen and courtiers, moving from sultan to sultan in search of hospitality and employment. In the circumstances, the class of intellectuals which they represented was more of a clique. This became apparent in the large number of Jews concerned. Solomon ben-Gabirol (Avicebron, Avencebrol) in the eleventh century was the first philosopher of note in the Maghrib. In the twelfth, Ibn Maymun (Maimonides) ranked with Ibn Rushd. The association of this very distinct community with these branches of knowledge helped to establish them as the preserve of a minority.

The philosophers and natural scientists were certainly an élite. Although the accusation levelled at Ibn Rushd that he preferred reason to faith was inaccurate, there is no doubt that like Hayy ibn Yaqzan (Ibn Tufayl's fictional natural philosopher), he thought faith was for the people, its understanding in the light of reason the privilege of an intellectual aristocracy. The extent of their isolation was revealed at the height of their achievement in the second half of the twelfth century. Ibn Maymun was driven by Almohad persecution of the Jews to seek refuge in Cairo, where he became physician to no less a person than the sultan, the great Saladin, chivalrous opponent of Richard the Lionheart. Twenty years later at the death of the Almohad caliph Abu Ya'qub, Ibn Rushd fell from favour. Although briefly reconciled to the caliph Abu Yusuf al-Mansur, his last years were spent under attack from the partisans of the more orthodox doctrine of continuous creation.

Active intolerance of this kind was unusual. From the second half of the thirteenth century, with the collapse of the Almohad empire and the annexation of the bulk of Andalus by Portugal, Castile and Aragon, pressure of a very different kind was applied. The courts of North Africa and Granada, splendid as they might be, were now in competition with Seville in its new position as capital of a great Christian kingdom. The process in evidence at the fall of Toledo in 1085, when the astronomer al-Zarqali was induced by Alfonso VI to return to the city, came to a head under Alfonso the Wise in the 1250s, 60s and 70s. His monument, the Alfonsine Tables of the planetary movements compiled for him by the Jews Judah Cohen and Isaac Hazan, summed up the centuries of Arabic astronomy in a work which provided astronomers down to Galileo and his successors with an indispensable tool. The *Tables* stand for the systematic patronage of Arabic learning by the kings of Aragon as well as Castile, just as Idrisi's *Book of Roger* represents that of the kings of Sicily.

The chief beneficiaries of this Christian patronage were the Jews, who for over two hundred years maintained the tradition of the philosophers in Spain. They owed their encouragement to the fact that their wealthy and educated community, being separated from both Christian subjects and Muslim enemies, was useful without being dangerous to Christian rulers. For their part, Muslims such as the traveller Ibn Battuta preferred to go east. The philosopher-historian Ibn Khaldun rejected the invitation of Pedro of Castile to return to the family homeland in Seville, and when defeated by political and academic opponents at Tunis, emigrated to

Above: The Jewish quarter of Seville. The Jews were expelled from the Spanish Kingdom in 1492, the year in which Granada was taken. Their architecture developed in the Mudejar fashion, resulting in several handsome synagogues, until they fell victim to the new intolerance which marked the nation-building of the united monarchy of Ferdinand and Isabella.

Above right: The arms of Portugal are displayed on this representation of the ocean-going sailing-ship, the type of vessel required by the Portuguese to explore the west coast of Africa on their way to the Indies. The lustreware bowl was made by the Mudejar potters of Manises near Valencia, where Muslim craftsmen worked for a Christian nobleman early in the fifteenth century.

Cairo. For him the journey was a tragedy, for two years later his family, coming to join him, was lost at sea. For the Arabic West his departure in 1382 seems like the end of an age. The fifteenth century by comparison was blank.

Working for the kings of Aragon, the Jews of Majorca meanwhile gave the picture of the world a wholly new clarity in the *portolans*, maps of the Mediterranean which by compass-bearings plotted on a chart gave the first accurate outlines of the coasts. Developed by Abraham Cresques to produce a map of the world, the principle of the portolan entered into the preparations of Prince Henry the Navigator of Portugal for the last and greatest triumph of the old doctrine of the round earth at the centre of the universe, the discovery of the sea routes to the Indies and the New World. But the future of Arabic philosophy and natural science had in fact been decided before the days of Ibn Khaldun and his friend the physician vizier Lisan al-Din ibn al-Khatib. The vagaries of opinion and opportunity to which they were subjected in their homeland contrasted with the scope for enquiry in Europe beyond the Pyrenees. More than a patron, Ibn Khaldun lacked a public to which his ideas could be addressed; in its absence, his works waited until the nineteenth century until they were discovered in the libraries of the Middle East. In his lifetime, the second half of the fourteenth century, his predecessors were already, in their exotic Latin form, names with which to conjure in the schools of Paris and Oxford, Padua and Prague: Abulcasis, Abenragel, Avencebrol, Arzachel; Avenzoar, Avempace, Abentofal, Alpetragius; Maimonides, Averroes, and many more. A rage for knowledge ensured that they were studied, taught and debated, not by the few but by the many who presented themselves for education in the multiplying universities of the later Middle Ages. Out of the argument, on the one hand narrowly technical, on the other broadly speculative, came the theories which had eluded the Arab thinkers, but in the seventeenth century resulted in the scientific revolution of the modern world.

WAR
AND PEACE

'*As the Commander of the Muslims bore down upon Ecija at the head of his victorious army, with all the booty God had granted him, the warning came that Don Nuño was approaching with the Christian host. Therefore he summoned the shaykhs of the Banu Marin, to consult with them how best to meet the infidels when the People saw the lines of the Christian cavalry coming on in thousands upon thousands, and the infantry in front of them rank upon rank, and in their midst the Nazarene captain, Don Nuño Gonzalez de Lara. Accursed, he advanced to war upon the Commander of the Muslims, under the shadow of the banners and the long trumpets that flapped and throbbed above his head, in the black night of battle surging onwards like the raging sea.*'[1]

So Satan himself might bring the hosts of hell to war upon the sons of God. The shape of the Castilian army, the infantry surrounding the knights until the time of the massed charge, is seen as it was intended to be seen, as a thing of terror. Prayer alone could ensure the triumph of right over such might:

> Alighting from his steed, [the Commander of the Muslims] washed his hands and face, his head and feet, bowed twice, and with uplifted hands prayed as the Prophet, God bless him and save him, prayed for the band of brothers who fought at the battle of Badr long ago, while the army supported his cry. Then mounting, he drew up his forces and declared: 'Company of Muslims and fighters for the faith, this is a tremendous day. Paradise has indeed opened its doors and adorned its comrades for you. Put all you have into the struggle with those who deny the Oneness of God, for whoever dies shall die a martyr, and whoever lives shall live in success, reward and praise. Therefore be strong and steadfast in your ranks, and trust in God that you may prosper!' And when they heard this, their spirits were ready for martyrdom, and they embraced each other in farewell, hearts beating, hearts breaking.[2]

But, said the chronicler, as God had answered the prayer of Muhammad in that most famous battle of Islam, giving victory against all odds, so

Within the cemetery of Chellah outside Rabat, the garden of the other world is adumbrated by the ancient trees. The dead, wrapped in white, lie on their right sides facing towards Mecca. On the Day of Judgment they will rise, swarming like locusts, to learn their final destiny.

now He favoured His people in battle against this latest in the long line of foes:

> Their voices went up in a shout for God Who is Most Great. As battle was joined and the fighting grew fierce, there was nothing to be seen but the arrows that fell like piercing meteors in endless torment on the foes of the Most High; the swords that ran with blood, and the heads of the infidels chopped and lopped from their bodies. For the champions of the Banu Marin wrought upon them like the lion of the forest, judging them by the sword, and giving them to taste the bitterness of death. So God gave victory to His army and triumph to His followers, as the captain of the infidels, Don Nuño, was killed, and his troops and his armies fled. The Commander of the Muslims ordered the heads of those killed to be cut off and counted, to the number of some eighteen thousand. Then the sultan reviewed his troops, looking for those who had perished in the fray. And of those who by God's will had found a happy release, the seal of the martyr, there were nine of the Banu Marin and fifteen of the Arabs and the men of Andalus, and eight of the volunteers.[3]

The Moors ride out to war beneath their characteristic war-flags (above). They are lightly armoured but extremely mobile by comparison with the Christian knights in their suits of chain mail who surround James the Conqueror, King of Aragon, as he prepares for the conquest of Majorca (below right). Both details are taken from frescoes in Barcelona depicting the invasion and conquest of the island.

It is just possible to see in this account the regular battle order of the Muslims, in which the infantry of kneeling spearmen and archers received the charge of the enemy until the opportunity came for their own cavalry to dash, draw back, and dash in again. Inferiority in weight to the more heavily armoured Christians was not considered a disadvantage; at some time in the fourteenth century the army of Granada abandoned its reliance on heavy armament for the sake of mobility and speed. But the ritual significance of the event, and the poetic associations of the action, eclipse the mundane technicalities. It is only in the aftermath that the victory is placed in context:

> The Commander of the Muslims wrote of the victory to the faithful throughout Andalus and North Africa, and his letters were read in the pulpits as the whole of the Muslim West rejoiced. The people celebrated, giving alms and freeing their slaves in thanks to God Most High, while the Commander of the Muslims came with the booty and the captives to Algeciras. Shackled and bound in chains and fetters, the champions and the chiefs of the Christians were led before him. As for Don Nuño, his head was sent by the Commander of the Muslims to Ibn al-Ahmar, the ruler of Granada. But Ibn al-Ahmar took the head and embalmed it in musk and camphor, and sent it to Alfonso to ingratiate himself with the king. Meanwhile the Commander of the Muslims remained at Algeciras to partition the booty which God had vouchsafed to him, taking the lawful fifth for the treasury, and dividing the rest among the fighters in the holy war. And the number of cattle therein was a hundred and twenty-four thousand, while the sheep were beyond count, one of them selling in Algeciras for a single piece of silver. The number of captives, men, women and children, was seven thousand eight hundred and thirty, that of the horses fourteen thousand, and of the mules and donkeys six hundred thousand. As for the armour and the swords and the pieces of equipment, they were too numerous to reckon. So the hands of the Muslims were filled and their fortunes made, while the Commander of the Muslims gave his portion to all and sundry, high and humble, noble and slave.[4]

The battle had in fact been the climax of a great cattle drive up and down the valley of the Guadalquivir, in which the raiders had successfully beaten off the pursuit. In doing so they had triumphantly added to their store of livestock, animal and human. By 1275, the year of this great success, the expedition was a belated example of the great campaigns which once had scoured the central plateaux of the Iberian peninsula. After the disappearance of the old battlefields, now far away in the north, the new line of conflict was settling around the foothills of the Sierra Nevada, the last redoubt of Muslim Spain. The prospect of plunder continued to appeal to a people in need of revenge.

Spiritual merit, gained in battle with the forces of unbelief, had on this occasion been amply rewarded with the attainment of all the material objects of the enterprise. Glut on this scale may have ruined the market; it was a magnificent bounty. The Marinid sultan Abu Yusuf could glory in his openhandedness. His power, as he transported his prisoners back to work upon the great mosque of New Fes, was finally secure. Abroad, the letters which proclaimed his success established his prestige. The head of Don Nuño was a still more pointed communication. Intended to shame the ruler of Granada, it became the instrument of Ibn al-Ahmar's own diplomacy. The gift of the trophy to Alfonso was not extraordinary. A Christian could just as easily be an ally as an enemy. Eight or nine years later, Abu Yusuf himself was intervening in the affairs of Castile on behalf of its king. Holy war had served its turn, and the great victory of 1275 was no obstacle to relations of a different kind.

Such attitudes had their counterparts among the Alfonsos and the Jameses, the Sanchos and Ferdinands, Garcias and Ramons. St James the Greater, Santiago Matamoros, 'Slayer of the Moors', was the heavenly

horseman with whose divine assistance they had reconquered the land of Andalus. As the pilgrims wore his badge of a scallop shell all the way to the shrine of Compostela, the saint's protection extended outwards to the battle against the false prophet of Islam. His knights, one of the three monastic orders established in the twelfth century, took from their enemies that dedication to the holy war contained in the word *ribat*. Ribat, indeed, appeared in Spanish as *rebato*, a form of raid, in which the Christians copied the Arab style of riding *a la jinete*, with short stirrups and a low saddle which allowed for quick manoeuvre. Major campaigns became crusades for the whole of European Christendom. That Far Bank of Andalus, where the Faithful fought with the sea at their backs to preserve the foothold of Islam across the Mediterranean, was a place of duty to the Cross. Thus of Chaucer's Knight:

> *In Gernade at the seege eek hadde he be*
> *Of Algezir, and riden in Belmarye.*[5]

Belmarye is Banu Marin, Banu Marin stands for Morocco; in the haze of a foreign language the human enemy dissolved. Creatures of legend took the place of reality. On the battlefield, instead of the Moorish champions, the giant Farragut, a grotesque Goliath, waited for his David.

Roland, dying, calling on his horn for the hosts of the emperor to return against the Saracen horde, was an archetype; the *Chanson de Roland* was a myth of good and evil. Even in legend, the Cid was more equivocal in his dealings with the Islamic foe. In life, his religion had been no obstacle to his career as a warrior in Muslim Spain. Navarre in the tenth century had become a constant ally of the caliphate at Cordova; its formidable Queen Theuda had her grandson Sancho cured of his fatness by the caliph's Jewish physician, Hasday ben Shaprut, and had him installed as King of Leon with the help of a large Muslim army. Some thirty years later the King of Navarre, Sancho II Garces, gave his daughter in marriage to the great Almanzor; Sanchuelo, 'Little Sancho', was the name given to their son. Coming to Almanzor's palace of al-Zahira outside Cordova, the king kissed the baby's foot and hand in token of submission. When Sanchuelo perished in the revolt which destroyed the empire of the caliphs in 1009–10, it was the turn of Navarre to levy tribute on Muslim Spain. In the long intervals thereafter, between the major wars and the rare moments of Christian conquest, treaties were the norm.

Treaties were contracts between parties each of whom recognized the other. Whether they recognized each other as equals, as superiors or inferiors, it was right and proper to identify themselves in the preambles to their correspondence and their agreements. In these preambles, where Muslims and Christians were concerned, Christ and Muhammad were valid alternatives; mutual respect in the name of the One God was required. In 1183 the Almohad caliph received a letter:

> To the most excellent and serene lord Joseph, elmire elmomini, king of kings and lord of lords, amir of all amirs, from Ubaldus, archbishop of Pisa, primate of Sardinia and legate of the Holy See, together with the consuls, councillors and all the citizens of Pisa, his most faithful servants, devoted service; may God in His great mercy defend, protect and keep him!
> We, your most faithful friends, hold your peace and friendship above all other, and desire to serve your Highness in everything. Since we are your faithful servants, having in you the greatest hope

and trust, we are much astonished that in your realm of Bougie [Bijaya, on the Algerian coast], our people have been stopped from exporting leather, and when they have come have been detained, and prevented from leaving when they wished. For which reason we ask your Magnificence, that you should treat our people as well as you are accustomed to do, and if it pleases, instruct your officers at Bougie that they should not stop the Pisans trading in leather or in any other goods, but should let them go freely from your land whenever they wish, that we may express our greatest thanks to your Highness.[6]

In such language business was done.

At Tunis the treaty of peace concluded with the French Crusaders after the death of King Louis at the siege of the city in 1270, established a comprehensive and wholly typical relationship between Muslim and Christian rulers and their subjects. Item by item, all Muslims from the territories belonging to the Hafsid prince al-Mustansir, going into any of the lands of the King of France and his allies, were to be safe from attack by land and sea, or restitution would be made; so too if they were shipwrecked. Likewise all Christians in the lands of the amir would go under the protection of God for their persons and their property, so long as they were about their business, enjoying all conditions made in favour of their kings and their counts, and abiding by their own customs; all debts to them would be honoured. Neither Muslims nor Christians would aid each other's enemies; all prisoners were to be exchanged. The Crusaders were to leave at once. In return, they were to be paid 210,000 ounces of gold (nearly 6 tonnes), each ounce worth fifty pieces of silver. The treaty, whose various texts in the various languages had been expertly scrutinized and witnessed, was to last for fifteen solar years. An extraordinary provision was the right of residence and worship at Tunis granted to monks and priests, while a final clause satisfied the claims of Charles, Count of Anjou, in his capacity as King of Sicily: five years' back payment of the tribute formerly paid to the Emperor Frederick II, and double the amount per year in future.

The opposition nevertheless remained. The principle was invariable, the distinction between people on the grounds of religion, and the fundamental separation of their communities. No agreement could abolish from the mind its consciousness of the difference. That consciousness proved in the end unbearable when it was a question of the subjects of a Muslim or a Christian state. For the dwindling number of Christians under Muslim rule and for the Mudejars – the large Muslim populations of Sicily and Spain who had been *mudajjan*, 'tamed' by the Christian conquests – the terms of toleration were handed down by the sovereign nation. Eventually they were revoked. Conversion or expulsion, voluntary or involuntary, was the fate of many if not most of the surviving Christians of Andalus and North Africa, just as it eventually became the hard choice for Muslims and for Jews in the Spanish kingdoms. Against such a background, guarded contacts at home and abroad were the most that were ever achieved.

If there is a word to express the barrier between the religious communities, and what passed across from one to the other within the limits of law and convention, it is *diwan*. An Arabic word of Persian origin, it may variously mean a couch, an assembly of people in council, a collection of poems, an official register or a government ministry. The diwan or ministry encountered by the merchant arriving from abroad was the customs, whence diwan passed into Spanish as *aduana*, into Italian

Above: Lustreware bowl of the first half of the fourteenth century from Malaga; the name is written on the base. In the period of the Nasrid kingdom of Granada, Malaga became the centre of an important ceramic industry. The tradition of lustreware, in which oxides of silver, copper and iron were dissolved in vinegar to give the effect of gold, was imported from Egypt in the tenth century (see page 37). Although the industry passed in the fifteenth century from Malaga to the Mudejar centre of Manises (Valencia), the manufacture of this Malagan ware spread to Italy under the name maiolica ('Malaga'), and from there to France under the name faïence (from Faenza, one of the several Italian towns where it was made).

Opposite: Ceremonial sword of iron, with a hilt of brass, from Granada in the early fourteenth century.

as *dogana*, and into French as *douane*. Through it the sultan controlled the different nationalities, each one in its own house, inn or factory, supervising their dealings and levying the agreed duty. Thus the governments of Tunis and Tlemcen, for example, grew rich on the exports of wool, wax, leather and gold in exchange for the manufactures of Italy and France. As Bougie, Bijaya provided the French word for a wax candle. The Marinids gave their name to the merino sheep; introduced at the end of the thirteenth century, the breed brought a new kind of prosperity to the ruined farmlands of al-Andalus.

Technical terms like diwan have passed extensively into Spanish and Portuguese, revealing something of the innovations and achievements of the Arabs in the western Mediterranean from the eighth century onwards. The styles and skills which they imposed upon the native architecture of the lands they conquered spread outwards into France and Italy at the

hands of Mozarab and Moorish craftsmen and their imitators. At Le Puy, one of the greatest gathering-points for the pilgrimage to Santiago de Compostela, the façade of the cathedral echoes the arcading of the Great Mosque of Cordova, the bays of the nave the domes of Ifriqiya. The lute, the instrument of the mediaeval troubadour, is *al-'ud*, 'the wood'.

Attempts to claim more, an Arabic origin and inspiration for the songs of the troubadours and the ideal of courtly love in the chivalrous society of Europe from the time of Richard Coeur-de-Lion to that of the *Morte d'Arthur* in the fifteenth century, have largely failed. The work of translation from the Arabic, evidence of which is required to prove direct influence as distinct from mere similarity, was almost wholly concentrated on the rendering of the books of science and philosophy into Latin. At Salerno in the eleventh century one of the last of the native Christians of Carthage, Constantine the African, translated a medical treatise. At Toledo in the twelfth century, the Italian Gerard of Cremona was the most prolific of the scholars from all over Europe who devoted themselves to the recovery of that wisdom of the Greeks which the Arabs had acquired. Robert of Ketton, Adelard of Bath, Robert of Chester, Michael the Scot, all contributed to a vast operation which in the course of a hundred years or so made Rhazes and Alpharabius, Avicenna and Averroes the commonplaces of Latin learning, then wound itself up, until in the fourteenth and fifteenth centuries the knowledge of Arabic which had been acquired for the purpose had vanished from the world of western European scholarship. A cultural diwan had selected and rejected with remarkable efficiency.

Nothing at all came of the attempt to offer something in return. Robert of Ketton had translated the Koran in the hope of learning the essence of the rival faith. A hundred years later, in the course of the thirteenth century, the preaching of Christianity to the Muslim world was undertaken on the basis of that knowledge. Those monks and priests allowed by the treaty of 1270 to live and worship at Tunis were missionaries, some preoccupied with the ransoming of captives, others more concerned to present their beliefs. From the time when five Franciscans were put to death at Marrakesh in 1220, they had run a grave risk. Some courted martyrdom, hoping to set the supreme example to people who would not listen to words alone. Most preferred a more cautious approach under cover of the agreements negotiated by Christian rulers, trying to draw the wise men of the Shari'a into argument. Raymond Lull, a Majorcan from the reconquered Balearics, and the hero of the whole enterprise, did both. Twice deported after the intercession of Christian merchants and Muslim scholars had saved him from death by stoning or incarceration at Tunis and Bijaya, he returned to Ifriqiya in 1314 to engage in controversy rather than public preaching. There he died, aged over eighty, stoned to death according to the legend, perhaps more simply from old age. Islam remained unconvinced.

The abysmal ignorance of the rival faith in Christian Europe, which persisted despite the activities of men like Raymond Lull, is typified by the rumour of an idol called Baphomet worshipped in the secret depths of the mosque. Yet hearsay, outside the realm of theology and ritual, was not without positive influence. In matters of literature, it provided a broad background to the occasional versions of Arabic stories which did appear in translation. In the mediaeval romance of Aucassin and Nicolette, the young knight Aucassin in search of his beloved upon the banks of the Rhone, is none other than al-Qasim. Oral transmission reinforced, even if it did not account for, the similarities of poetic sentiment and popular anecdote between the *Roman de la Rose* and the

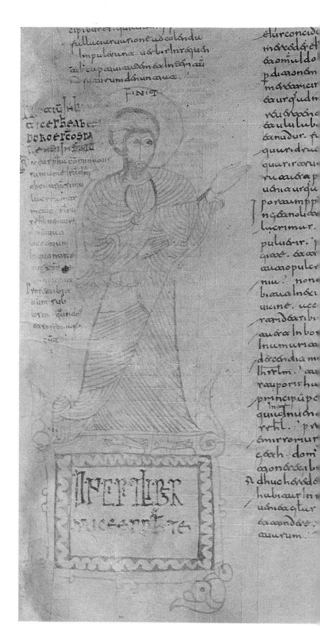

The prophet Miqueas; a pen drawing of a turbanned figure with a halo, from an illustrated Bible of the Mozarabic community in the tenth century. Copies of traditional texts apart, these 'would-be Arabs' were accustomed to use the Arabic script, in which they wrote the Romance vernacular they shared with the Muslim population. The equally Arabized Jewish community meanwhile employed the Hebrew alphabet for the writing of Arabic. Like the Jews, the Mozarabs led a separate existence as an urban community distinguished from their Muslim neighbours on the grounds of religion. They were governed by their own law under their own officials, with a special representative at the court of the caliph.

Candlestick from Elvira, the town immediately to the west of Granada, which took its name from the Roman and Visigothic city of Illiberis; it was eclipsed by Granada in the eleventh century, when a Berber dynasty of 'Little Kings' built its fortress capital on the hill across from the Alhambra. In this curious piece of metalwork, a hexagonal turret stands upon twelve columns; six birds perch upon its battlements. The so-called 'stepped merlons' of the crenellation, with their triangular shape and zigzag sides, are found for example on the walls of the Great Mosque of Cordova; the form, which became a regular motif of tilework as well as building, is of Middle Eastern origin and derived from the shape of a plant. Above the turret, the shaft of the spike is furnished with a plate perforated with the design of a six-pointed star.

Arabic odes, the *Decameron of Boccaccio* and the *Thousand and One Nights.* And when poetry took over the expression of theology, common ground was found at the heart of the two distinct cultures.

Again there is no documentary proof of borrowing. Dante, when he composed his *Divine Comedy* of a journey down through Hell and up through Purgatory into Paradise, may never have read the little *Book of the Ladder*, a description of the nocturnal journey of Muhammad through heaven and hell, when it was translated into Spanish and French. When he created the figure of Beatrice, the earthly love for whose sake he was guided, by God's grace, through the perils and pains of the afterlife to the ultimate bliss, he cannot have known the poetry of the mystic Ibn al-'Arabi. Nevertheless, the way taken by the Florentine author out of the dark wood of the world, in which the right road was lost, had already been found in the writings of the Muslim.

Chaste love, the passion of the self-denying lover by which the narrator of the *Divine Comedy* was redeemed, was a commonplace of Arabic poetry and of Christian romance. It was a paradox which, for the Arabic poet who set his eyes on heaven, was especially acute. The Garden of Paradise was filled with the loveliness of women whose enjoyment on earth was circumscribed by the Law of God. Aesthetics could express but not solve the problem they had created of a beauty so great that its attraction had to be resisted:

> *Willing as she was to couple, I refrained;*
> *the devil in her failed to be obeyed.*
> *Naked in the dark, her charm revealed, the veil*
> *of night itself was raised and swept aside.*
> *Curtaining my lust with the divine command,*
> *within my bounds of abstinence I stayed,*
> *Lying with her thirsty as the camel calf*
> *that cannot suckle with its muzzle tied.*
> *Nothing in that garden for the like of me*
> *but sight and scent of its delights arrayed;*
> *Member of no herd, no wandering ox was I*
> *to pasture on the flowers of the glade.*[7]

To the figure of Ibn Zaydun lamenting the departure and unfaithfulness of the love he had once enjoyed, was added that of Abu 'l-Bahr sighing over his refusal to possess a loveliness like that of the new moon when it shone for him.

> *Lovers are at a loss in love,*
> *caught in its contradictions.*[8]

These words of Ibn al-'Arabi, written at Mecca in the first years after his departure from al-Andalus, were the starting-point of his own spiritual journey, in which the halts of the qasida, the classical ode, became the stopping-places of the spirit on the way to God. His Beatrice, his inspiration and his guide, was the daughter of the man who taught him wisdom. Nizam, Eye of the Sun and the Splendour, dazzling in her radiance, gave a glimpse of the heavenly beauty which flashed like lightning on the earth, and as quickly vanished. Only the memory might remain of an unutterable loss, a moment of union with the divine for which a man might seek for the rest of his life and rarely if ever find again. That supreme ecstasy, beyond any physical consummation, was the ultimate gift of God to those who bent their minds and hearts upon Him.

Muhyi al-Din ibn al-'Arabi was a Sufi, a 'woolly man' – the name comes from the characteristic dress of the ascetic. He represented a mysticism which by the time he left Spain in 1201 at the age of thirty-eight had condensed into doctrines, prayers and devotions handed down, like the Law itself, from master to pupil. Contemplatives of his kind were far away from the ferocity of the Almoravids, the Men of the Ribat, although their origin as holy men was much the same. The pious 'Ali, son of Yusuf ibn Tashfin, had burnt the books of the theologian al-Ghazzali, one of which, the *Ihya' 'Ulum al-Din* or 'Bringing to Life of the Sciences of Religion', had tried to reconcile the teachings of the Sufis with the Shari'a. Muhyi al-Din, 'He Who Brings Religion to Life', was nevertheless brought up to the path of Sufism in the Spain of the philosophers, of Ibn Bajja and Ibn Tufayl. As he moved through the seven stages along the way, repentance, abstinence, renunciation, poverty, patience, trust in God and final satisfaction, his thought was cast in the mould of a universe which was itself a revelation and a reflection of the divine. Meditation proceeded from the Sura of Light, the chapter of the Koran which includes the verse:

God is the light of the heavens and of the earth. The likeness of His light is that of a niche or a chandelier in which is a lamp, the lamp in a glass, the glass like a brilliant star, lit from a blessed tree, an olive neither eastern nor western, whose oil would shine almost without the touch of fire. Light upon light. God guides to His light those whom He wishes, speaking to humanity in metaphor, He who knows all.[9]

'OH GOD, bless and save our lord and master MUHAMMAD and the family of our lord MUHAMMAD, to whom is all refuge and recourse; OH GOD, bless and save our lord and master MUHAMMAD and the family of our lord MUHAMMAD, the stamp and seal of the divine message; OH GOD, bless and save our lord and master MUHAMMAD and the family of our lord MUHAMMAD, the omen and the sign; OH GOD . . .' The Dala'il al-khayrat, or The Signs of Blessings, a book of prayers in the name of the Prophet composed by the Moroccan saint and mystic al-Jazuli in the fifteenth century. The endless repetition of the same formula with its systematic variations is a verbal equivalent of the arabesque; when spoken, the words empty the mind of all except God. The book was widely used; in this copy the words 'Oh God' and 'Muhammad' are written in gold to produce a visual pattern. Al-Jazuli was a preacher who toured Morocco at the head of his crowd of followers; after his death they carried his body about the country. His teaching was maintained by his disciples, who formed the Sufi brotherhood of the Jazuliya.

117

It was a Muslim meditation. Ibn al-'Arabi did not follow Hayy ibn Yaqzan, Ibn Tufayl's fictional castaway, into a realm of mind which dispensed with the need for revelation, and hence for the religion of scripture. For him, the awful gap between the Creator and His creation opened between the soul and its passing away into God. The metaphor of the qasida, evoking a journey through the wilderness from the desolation of parting to the gladness of meeting, was a means of expression for the tenuous and fragile way across.

The poetry is difficult. It required a commentary from the author to explain its meaning to his readers. That same commentary is needed for a translation, to render the images into English and to make them intelligible. Each one is a symbol, to be understood against the background of Islam, its theology and its literature. The camels which in the classical ode rise at dawn to leave the encampment empty in the waste are the actions which a man performs by the will of God. Upon their backs, hidden in the howdahs, they carry away the maidens who are the spirits of those actions, the intentions of the actor which have stamped them as his own for good or evil. Let the intentions be good, and these spirits are his darlings, leaving him behind as they set out upon their way to heaven with no more than a glimpse of their beauty through the curtains. Their piercing loveliness is a wonder greater than he can bear, a revelation of the Divine Wisdom which rules the world. That Wisdom is described as Bilqis, the Queen of Sheba, whose appearance to Muhammad on his journey through the celestial spheres had caused his guide in the story, the angel Gabriel, to faint before such a disclosure on the part of God. Bilqis, child of genie and woman, spirit and flesh, comes from the Koran. At first proud and independent, she submitted to God when in the course of her confrontation with Sulayman (Solomon) she mistook a floor of glass for a sheet of water, lifting her dress before she realized what it was. Personifying in this way the divine being and its reflection in the world, Bilqis became for Ibn al-'Arabi the crux of his desire. It was through her that a man might pass at the moment of death from fragmentation in the phenomenal to absorption in the real:

> *The day they left, the camels did not go*
> > *without the peacocks on their backs, resplendent girls,*
> *With eyes that kill, as angels in their power,*
> > *appearing each as Bilqis on her throne of pearls.*
> *When Sheba walks within the hall of glass,*
> > *you see a sun whose sphere a master whirls;*
> *Her voice shall raise the dead her looks have slain,*
> > *as Jesus brought them to the summons of his calls;*
> *Bright Torah, tablet smooth, the legs which I*
> > *like Moses follow as the hands withdraw the veils;*
> *Ecclesiastic, stripped of ornament,*
> > *upon her shines the light that perfect goodness rules;*
> *Untamed, alone in her own heart, a tomb*
> > *reminds her of her solitude with marble walls;*
> *Beyond the comprehension of the wise,*
> > *of rabbi, priest she is, or master of the schools;*
> *Her finger on the Gospels as the truth*
> > *would make us bishops, mitred, in their copes and palls.*
> *The day they left, upon the road, the flag*
> > *above the armies of my fortitude unfurls;*
> *Oh may that loveliness blow on the wind*
> > *to me, when to my throat in death my spirit curls;*

Then, keep me from the thought that I may be
  my God, the last illusion of the Fiend for souls;
I cried out when her camel rose to go,
  'Driver, don't take her from me, far upon the hills!' [10]

In his own *Nocturnal journey to the highest of all*, Ibn al-'Arabi takes the Mi'raj or ascent of Muhammad from Jerusalem to the throne of God as a more elaborate vehicle of his thought than the qasida could ever be. Here and elsewhere in an immense output of writing, he develops the allusions of the verse on a scale to match the theme. Intensity remains. As the heavens drop away, the philosopher, like Dante's Virgil, is obliged to halt. Only the believer goes on. God takes His creature back into the everlasting vision.

The vision returned to earth. Al-Khadir, 'the Green', was the equivalent of St James of Compostela among the Christians of Spain as the patron saint of Islam in the west. Presiding over the ends of the earth and the surrounding sea, he symbolized the furthest frontier of the Muslim world. He it was who gave God's blessing to the holy war upon the unbeliever, and victory to the fighter for the faith. The murabitun, the men of the ribat, fought in his battle to defend the borders of the true religion. At the same time he brought illumination to mankind, sometimes to the unbeliever, more especially to the holy man of God. Under his auspices the murabit, the fierce warrior, became contemplative. As Sufism spread in the west, the contemplative way of life evolved. By the thirteenth century the ribat was the *zawiya*, 'the niche', the retreat of the holy man from which the light of God streamed out to the people. As Andalus was lost, the zawiya grew.

A zawiya was built around its founder's tomb. A mosque was provided for prayer. A school, refectory and living-quarters enabled the holy man and his disciples to live and meditate together. Spiritually and materially it was a household built upon hospitality. The shaykh, the holy man, 'spread a table'; his pupils ate as well as read under him. They were of all ages, from boys to men, as many as a hundred at a time. The servants and their families might be as many again. Guests were continually entertained, while the poor of the neighbourhood could expect regular charity. It was an exercise in redistribution, for the zawiya itself was maintained by pious gifts, sometimes of property which provided a regular income, sometimes of food and other necessities. This was more laudable. Ideally the inmates lived by divine providence, from hand to mouth. The shaykh al-Jadidi at Kairouan in the fourteenth century was accustomed to make once a year a large bowl of sweetstuff with butter, flour, honey, fruit and nuts. One year there was no butter, when at the very last moment a man came in quite unawares from a village miles away with a donkey load. The dish was made, and the bowl placed in the middle of the court, so that all who entered might eat. For the Muslim that was just as it should be.

My soul says to me: Death has come for you
  in all your sins, a sea of turbulence,
With nothing for the road. I say, Be still;
  provisions to the door of Providence? [11]

Nothing is known of the purpose of the halls of the Alhambra in the daily life of the monarch and his court; their function is for the most part unclear. They have a strong intellectual structure, both as works of art and as monuments to the glory of the princes who built them. But the life of which they were the shell is obscure. Legend has colonized them, telling tales of captive princesses, murdered men, ladies in love and kings in council. These are substitutes for knowledge. Keen intelligence and great skill have gone into the construction of this little pavilion which juts out from the short eastern side of the Court of the Lions towards its counterpart at the far end. It forms a porch at the entrance to the Hall of the Kings, and an archway for the water rising and running in a channel across the floor out to the fountain in the middle of the court. In the Mosque of the Qarawiyin at Fes, two similar pavilions, identically placed at either end of the long courtyard, house fountains for the ritual ablution of the worshipper. In the Alhambra the function, if any, is lost. The symbolism alone remains.

NOTES

THE FRAMEWORK OF SOCIETY

1 Anon, *Dhakhīrat al-sanīya*, Ed. M. Ben Cheneb, Algiers, 1921, 186–8

2 *The Arts of Islam*, Catalogue of Exhibition, Hayward Gallery, 8 April – 4 July 1976, Arts Council of Great Britain, 1976, p.306, no.487

3 'Abd al-Wāḥid al-Marrakushī, *History of the Almohades*, Ed. R. P. A. Dozy, 2nd ed., Leiden, 1881, reprint Amsterdam, 1968, 239

4 Ibn Khaldūn, *Kitāb al-'Ibar*, Beirut, 1956–61, VII, 347

THE MUSLIM MIND

1 Koran, III, 21

2 Koran, XXII, 23

3 Ibn Nājī, *Ma'ālim al-īmān*, Tunis, AH 1320, 15–18, lines 1–18 (Ibn Rashīq)

4 *Inscriptions Kairouanaises*, Ed. B. Roy and P. Poinssot, Vol II, Fasc.2, Paris, 1958, p.502, no.363

5 Koran, LVII, 20

6 E. Lévi-Provençal, 'En relisant le "Collier de la Colombe"', *Al-Andalus*, XV, 2 (1950), 335–75, Appendix I, 361–2

7 Ibn Bassām, *Al-Dhakhīra fī maḥāsin ahl al-Jazīra*, Part IV, Vol. 1, Cairo, 1945, 231 (Anon)

THE ARAB MIND

1 Koran, I, 1–5

2 Ibn Bassām, *Al-Dhakhīra*, IV, 1, 182 (Ibn Sharaf)

3 *Ibid.*, 181 (Ibn Sharaf)

4 *Ibid.*, 168 (Ibn Sharaf)

5 *Ibid.* (Ibn Sharaf)

6 Ibn Sa'id, *El Libro de las Banderas de los Campeones*, Ed. and Spanish trans., E. Garcia Gomez, Madrid, 1942, 84; Eng. trans., A. J. Arberry, *An Anthology of Moorish Poetry*, Cambridge, 1953, 139 (for comparison); (Ibn al-Zaqqaq)

7 *Al-Dhakhīra*, IV, 1, 168 (Ibn Sharaf)

8 *Las Banderas*, 45; Arberry, 67 (Abu Hafs)

9 *Ibid.*, 33; 47 (Ibn Muqana)

10 *Ibid.*, 31; 42–3 (Ibn Jakha)

11 *Al-Dhakhīra*, IV, 1, 178 (Ibn Sharaf)

12 *Las Banderas*, 86; Arberry, 144 (Ibn Hariq)

13 *Al-Dhakhīra*, IV, 1, 181 (Ibn Sharaf)

14 *Las Banderas*, 43; Arberry, 63 (Ibn Shuhayd)

15 *Al-Dhakhīra*, IV, 1, 183–4 (Ibn Sharaf)

16 Al-'Umarī, *Masālik al-abṣār*, ms., Bibliothèque Nationale, Paris, no.2327, fo.44 vo. (Ibn Sharaf)

17 *Las Banderas*, 67; Arberry, 107 (Ibn Sa'id)

18 *Ibid.*, 84; 140 (Ibn al-Zaqqaq)

19 *Ibid.*, 88; 148 (Ibn Khafaja)

20 *Ibid.*, 62; 96 (Ibn Farsan)

21 *Ibid.*, 71; 114 (Ibn Sa'id)

22 *Ibid.*, 52; 79 (Al-Hajjam)

23 *Ibid.*, 19; 19 (Al-Liss)

24 Ibn 'Idhārī, *Kitāb al-Bayān al-Mughrib*, Ed. G. S. Colin and E. Lévi-Provençal, Vol II, Leiden, 1951, 227

25 *Al-Dhakhīra*, I, 1, 22

WAR AND PEACE

1 Ibn Abī Zar', *Rawd al-Qirtās*, lith. Fes, AH 1303, 228–30

2 *Ibid.*

3 *Ibid.*

4 *Ibid.*

5 Chaucer, *The Canterbury Tales*, Prologue, lines 56–7

6 De Mas Latrie, *Traites de paix et de commerce concernant les relations des chrétiens avec les Arabes de l'Afrique septentrionale au moyen-age*, Paris, 1866, 27

7 *Las Banderas*, 72–3; Arberry, 116 (Ibn Faraj)

8 Ibn al-'Arabī, *The Tarjumān al-Ashwāq; a collection of mystical odes*, Ed. and literal trans., R. A. Nicholson, Oriental Translation Fund, New Series, XX, Royal Asiatic Society, London, 1911, p. 15, no. 1, line 4; trans., 48

9 Koran, XXIV, 35

10 Ibn al-'Arabī, *Tarjumān*, pp. 15–16, no. 2; trans. and commentary, 49–53

11 *Las Banderas*, 99; Arberry, 163 (Al-Munsafi)

GLOSSARY

'abd slave, servant, worshipper; common in combination in proper names, e.g. 'Abd al-Rahman, 'Servant of the Merciful'

abu father; common in proper names, often indicating eldest son, e.g. Abu Yusuf Ya'qub, Jacob Father of Joseph

al- definite article, 'the'

'alim, pl. 'ulama' 'man of wisdom', scholar of the sciences of religion, basically the Islamic Law

Allah = al-ilah *The* God', i.e. God

almucantar = al-muqantar lit. 'vaulted, arched'; line of celestial latitude, engraved on astrolabe

amir leader, commander, ruler; title of ruler

Amir al-Mu'minin 'Commander of the Faithful'; title of caliph

Amir al-Muslimin 'Commander of the Muslims'; title of Almoravid and Marinid rulers

azimuth = al-samt lit. 'the way'; line of celestial longitude

banu sons; used for families, e.g. Banu Umayya, 'Sons of Umayya', Umayyads (see also **ibn**)

caliph = khalifa deputy, successor (of Muhammad as leader of the Muslim community; of the Mahdi Ibn Tumart in the case of the Almohads)

diwan variously, register; ministry; council; a poet's collected works

genie = jinn supernatural being, intermediate between angel and devil

hammam (Turkish) bathhouse

ibn son; used in patronymic, e.g. Ibn Khaldun, 'Son of Khaldun' (see also **banu**)

imam leader of congregation in prayer

Imam leader of the Muslim community; a title of the Fatimid caliph

islam submission

Islam submission (to God); the true faith

Koran = Qur'an 'that which is recited'; the Book of God

madrasa place of study; college; school

Mahdi 'The Rightly-Guided One' sent by God to bring heavenly justice back to earth

Maghrib The West; more narrowly, North Africa

Malikites followers of the Malikite school of the Law, one of the four orthodox, Sunnite schools, originating at Medina, and becoming dominant in the Muslim West

mihrab semi-circular niche in the long south or south-eastern wall of the prayer-hall of a mosque, indicating the direction in which the worshippers must face to pray

mosque = masjid 'place of worship'; a building principally for prayer

Mozarabs = musta'ribun 'would-be Arabs'; Christians living in Muslim Spain who spoke Arabic and lived in Arab fashion

Mudejars = mudajjan lit. 'tamed'; Muslims living under Christian rule in Spain after the Reconquista in the middle of the thirteenth century

muezzin = mu'adhdhin 'caller'; the crier who summons the faithful to pray

muhtasib lit. 'he who reckons or takes into account'; the official who supervised the market

mu'minun 'the faithful'; original name for Arab members of the community

murabit 'man of the ribat', fighter in the holy war, holy man

al-Murabitun = the Almoravids Saharan Berber nomads, followers of Ibn Yasin

musalla 'place of prayer'; open space outside city for mass worship and meeting

muslim 'one who submits'

Muslim 'one who submits to God'; a follower of Islam

al-Muwahhidun = the Almohads 'those who proclaim the Oneness of God'; Berbers of the High Atlas, followers of the Mahdi Ibn Tumart

Muwallads lit. 'adopted children'; Spanish Christians, beginning with the Visigothic nobility, who converted to Islam and became as Arabs

muwashshah lit. 'adorned'; a form of Arabic verse in Muslim Spain employing rhyme and refrains in the Spanish vernacular

qadi judge, judging by the Islamic Law

qasba = Alcazaba fortress, citadel

qasr = Alcazar fortress, palace

qasida ode; classical Arabic verse form

qayrawan 'caravan'; stopping place or camp for army, giving name to city of Qayrawan (Kairouan)

ribat 'garrison'; fortress for defence of Muslim frontier against infidel; dwelling-place of holy men; the holy war; dedication to the holy war

risala letter; title of résumé of Islamic Law according to Malikite doctrine by Ibn Abi Zayd

Shari'a the Islamic Law

shaykh elder; spiritual master

souk = suq market (place or street)

Sufi 'woolly man'; Muslim mystic

Sufism Muslim mysticism or devotionalism

sultan 'man of power', 'power'; ruler; state government

Sunna Custom (of the Prophet); the way of the Law according to the example of Muhammad

tiraz woven silk cloth; inscription embroidered on the cloth; factory where the cloth is made

al-'ud 'the wood'; lute

'ulama' pl. of 'alim, q.v.

umm mother; used in proper names in combination usually with name of firstborn son, e.g. Umm Mallal (Zirid princess)

'umran civilization

zajal form of verse in Muslim Spain, composed in colloquial Arabic

CHRONOLOGICAL TABLE

SPAIN (ANDALUS)	MOROCCO	IFRIQIYA
		*c.*670 Foundation of Kairouan
		700–5 Creation of province of Ifriqiya
711 Tariq conquers Spain		
732 Arabs defeated at Poitiers		
	739 Berber rebellions followed by Arab rebellions	
	750 Umayyads at Damascus overthrown by 'Abbasids	
755 Arrival of Umayyad 'Abd al-Rahman in Spain; Umayyad dynasty founded in Andalus	Berber rebels become independent	'Abbasids regain control of Ifriqiya from Arab rebels
778 Charlemagne attacks Saragossa	Fes founded by Idris-Idrisid dynasty established	
788 d 'Abd al-Rahman I successor son Hisham I		
796 d Hisham I; successor son Hakam I		
Series of rebellions in cities		800 Ibrahim ibn al-Aghlab founds Aghlabid dynasty
813 Emigration of rebels from Cordova to Fes, Ifriqiya, Egypt		
822 d Hakam I; successor son 'Abd al-Rahman II		Series of rebellions in cities, armies, before dynasty secure
		825 People emigrate from Kairouan to Fes
Strong influence of 'Abbasid fashions at court		827 Invasion of Sicily from Ifriqiya; conquest continues for 100 years
852 d 'Abd al-Rahman II; successor son Muhammad I		
Execution of Christian martyrs		
886 d Muhammad I; successor son al-Mundhir		
888 d al-Mundhir; successor brother 'Abd Allah		
		890s Arrival of Fatimid missionary Abu 'Abd Allah among Kutama peoples
Ibn Hafsun in Bobastro; Umayyad authority restricted to Cordova		909 Abu 'Abd Allah drives Aghlabids from Kairouan; 'Ubayd Allah al-Mahdi founds Fatimid dynasty of caliphs
912 d 'Abd Allah; successor grandson 'Abd al-Rahman III al-Nasir		
Umayyads gradually recover power		916 Foundation of Mahdia by Fatimids
927 Bobastro taken	War in northern Morocco between Umayyads and Fatimids, and between their Berber allies, continuing until end of 10th century	
928 'Abd al-Rahman III takes title of caliph (Commander of the Faithful)		
961 d 'Abd al-Rahman III; successor son Hakam II		
		969 Fatimids conquer Egypt
		972 Fatimid caliph moves to Cairo leaving Zirids as lieutenants in Ifriqiya
976 d Hakam II; successor infant son Hisham II Ibn Abi 'Amir Al-Mansur (Almanzor) becomes regent for Umayyads War on Christians of northern Spain		
1002 d Almanzor		
1009 Overthrow of Almanzor's son		
1013 Sack of Cordova		
1031 End of Umayyad dynasty Period of Little Kings, rulers of city states led by Seville		
	1040s Ibn Yasin forms Almoravids in Sahara, begins holy war	
		1048 Zirid Mu'izz repudiates Fatimids
		1052 Mu'izz defeated by Arab tribes of Banu Hilal, deserted by subjects
	1057 d Ibn Yasin; successor Abu Bakr	1057 Mu'izz abandons Kairouan for Mahdia
	*c.*1069 Abu Bakr founds Marrakesh, installs Yusuf ibn Tashfin	
	Almoravids under Yusuf conquer Morocco	Ifriqiya divided into city states, tribal territories
1085 Capture of Toledo by Castile, Muslims appeal to Almoravid Yusuf ibn Tashfin		

SPAIN (ANDALUS)	MOROCCO	IFRIQIYA
1086–90 Yusuf ibn Tashfin conquers Andalus, exiles Little Kings to Morocco		
1094 El Cid takes Valencia		
1099 El Cid besieged in Valencia Yusuf ibn Tashfin takes title 'Commander of the Muslims'; Andalus and Morocco united under Almoravids		
1106 d Yusuf ibn Tashfin, successor son Ali		
1118 Saragossa taken by King of Aragon		
	1120s Ibn Tumart forms Almohads in High Atlas	
	c.1130 d Ibn Tumart, succeeded by his caliph 'Abd al-Mu'min	
		1135 Djerba taken by Normans of Sicily
	c.1141 'Abd al-Mu'min begins campaign against Almoravids	
1143 d 'Ali ibn Yusuf ibn Tashfin, successor son Tashfin		
	1145 Almohads defeat Almoravids; d Tashfin	
		1146-9 Norman conquest of Tripoli, Gabes, Sfax, Mahdia, Sousse
1147 Almohads capture Seville; flight of Almoravid Ibn Ghaniya to Majorca; Andalus substantially independent; Ibn Mardanish ruler of Murcia	1147 Marrakesh captured by Almohads	
		1152 Almohad 'Abd al-Mu'min annexes Central Maghrib
		1159 Almohads conquer Ifriqiya, drive Normans from coastal cities
	1163 d 'Abd al-Mu'min, successor son Abu Ya'qub	
1172 Murcia taken by Almohad Abu Ya'qub. Andalus, Morocco and Ifriqiya united in Almohad empire, capitals Seville and Marrakesh		
1184 d Almohad Abu Ya'qub, successor son Abu Yusuf. Beginning of doctrinal controversy between Almohad caliph and Almohad shaykhs		
1195 Almohads defeat Castile at Alarcos		Invasion of Ifriqiya by Almoravids from Majorca
1199 d Almohad Abu Yusuf, successor son al-Nasir		
1203 Almohads conquer Majorca from Almoravids		
		1205-7 Defeat of Almoravids by Almohad al-Nasir; Abu Muhammad al-Hafsi made viceroy at Tunis
1212 Defeat of Almohads by Christians at Las Navas de Tolosa		
1213 d Almohad al-Nasir, successor son al-Mustansir		
1227 Murder of caliph al-'Adil; his brother al-Ma'mun repudiates Almohad doctrine, invades Morocco, massacres Almohad shaykhs, takes power at Marrakesh		
	Break-up of Almohad empire	
1230s Ibn Hud takes power in Andalus	Yaghmurasin takes power at Tlemcen, founds Ziyanid dynasty	Abu Zakariya' al-Hafsi assumes leadership of Almohads, founds Hafsid dynasty at Tunis
1236 Ferdinand of Castile takes Cordova Conquest of Algarve by Portugal, of Valencia by Aragon		
1248 Ferdinand takes Seville		
Ibn al-Ahmar, founder of Nasrid dynasty at Granada, becomes last Muslim ruler in Spain		
	1250 Marinid dynasty established at Fes	
		1270 St Louis, King of France, attacks Tunis on crusade
1275 Marinid Abu Yusuf invades Spain		
	1276 New Fes begun	
	1299– Siege of Tlemcen by Marinid ruler 1307 Abu Ya'qub	
	1331 Accession of Marinid Abu 'l-Hasan	
	1337 Marinids take Tlemcen	
1340 Christians defeat Marinids in Spain		
1344 Fall of Algeciras, expulsion of Marinids		
		1347 Marinid Abu 'l-Hasan conquers Ifriqiya
	1348 Rebellion of son Abu 'Inan	
	1351 d Abu 'l-Hasan, successor Abu 'Inan	
		1352-7 Marinid Abu 'Inan reconquers Ifriqiya
	1358 d Abu 'Inan; Marinid power weakened; Ziyanids recover Tlemcen	
1362–91 Reign of Nasrid Muhammad al-Ghani at Granada		Hafsids recover Ifriqiya
	1415 Portuguese take Ceuta	
	1458–91 Portuguese take Alcazarquivir, Tangier, Larache and Azemmour	
1479 Ferdinand and Isabella married		
1492 Christian monarchs conquer Granada		

BIBLIOGRAPHY

The following is a guide to the literature of the subject in English; the majority of books and articles are in French and Spanish. While it has not been possible to acknowledge all sources, Oleg Grabar's *The Alhambra* deserves special mention for its discussion of the ideas behind the construction of the palace fortress.

Abun-Nasr, J. *A History of the Maghrib*, 2nd ed., Cambridge 1975

Ahmed, Aziz *A History of Islamic Sicily*, Edinburgh 1975

Arberry, A. J. *Moorish Poetry*, Cambridge 1953

Battuta, Ibn *Travels in Asia and Africa, 1325–1354*, trans. and selected by H. A. R. Gibb, London 1929

Burckhardt, T. *Moorish Culture in Spain*, trans. A. Jaffa, London 1972

Cambridge History of Africa, vol. 2, c. 500 BC–AD 1050, Ed. J. D. Fage, Cambridge 1978, chapters 8, 10, 11; vol. 3. c. 1050 – c. 1600, Ed. R. Oliver, Cambridge, 1977, chapters 4, 5

Cambridge History of Islam, Ed. P. M. Holt, A. K. S. Lambton and B. Lewis, 2 vols., Cambridge 1970

Cheyne, A. *Muslim Spain; its History and Culture*, Minneapolis 1974

De Montêquin, F. *Compendium of Hispano-Islamic Art and Architecture*, St Paul, Minnesota 1976

Dozy, R. *Spanish Islam*, trans. G. G. Stokes, London 1913, reprint 1972

Encyclopaedia of Islam, 1st ed., Leiden and London 1913–38; 2nd ed., Leiden and London 1954–, in progress

Glick, T. H. *Islamic and Christian Spain in the Early Middle Ages*, Princeton 1979

Grabar, O. *The Alhambra*, London 1978

Hazm, Ibn *The Ring of the Dove*, trans. A. J. Arberry, London 1953

Hitti, P. K. *A History of the Arabs*, London 1937, many editions

Hole, E. *Andalus: Spain under the Muslims*, London 1958

Hopkins, J. F. P. *Mediaeval Muslim Government in Barbary*, London 1958

Irvine, Washington *A Chronicle of the Conquest of Granada*, London 1850

Issawi, C. *An Arab Philosophy of History*, London 1950

Jackson, G. *The Making of Mediaeval Spain*, London 1972

Julien, Ch.-A. *History of North Africa from the Arab Conquest to 1830*, Eng. Ed. and trans. C. C. Stewart and J. Petrie, London 1970

Khaldun, Ibn *The Muqaddimah: an Introduction to History*, trans. F. Rosenthal, 3 vols., 2nd ed., Princeton 1967

Landau, Rom *The Philosophy of Ibn 'Arabi*, London 1959

Lane-Poole, S. *The Moors in Spain*, London and New York 1889

Legey, F. *The Folklore of Morocco*, trans. L. Hoty, London 1935

Le Tourneau, R. *The Almohad Movement in North Africa in the twelfth and thirteenth century*, Princeton 1969

Le Tourneau, R. *Fez in the Age of the Marinids*, trans. B. A. Clement, Norman, Oklahoma 1961

Livermore, H. V. *History of Spain*, London 1958

Livermore, H. V. *The Origins of Spain and Portugal*, London 1971

Montgomery Watt, W. and Cachia, P. *A History of Islamic Spain*, Edinburgh 1965

Norris, H. T. *Saharan Myth and Saga*, Oxford 1972

Norwich, John Julius *The Kingdom in the Sun, 1130–1194*, London 1970

Norwich, John Julius *The Normans in the South, 1016–1130*, London 1967

O'Callaghan, J. F. *A History of Mediaeval Spain*, Ithaca and London 1975

Sordo, E. and Swaan, Wim *Moorish Spain*, London 1963

Southern, R. W. *Western Views of Islam in the Middle Ages*, Cambridge, Mass., 1962

Trimingham, J. Spencer *The Sufi Orders of Islam*, Oxford 1971

Whishaw, B. and E. M. *Arabic Spain: sidelights on her history and art*, London 1912

ACKNOWLEDGMENTS

Werner Forman and the publishers would like to acknowledge the help of the following museums and private collections in permitting the photography shown on the pages listed:
Biblioteca Nacional, Madrid: 16, 45, 94–95, 114, 115; Kunstgewerbemuseum, Berlin: 26; Mrs Bashir Mohamed collection, London: 14, 56, 74, 96, 117; Musée Archéologique, Tlemcen: 34 top, 34 bottom; Musée National du Bardo, Tunis: 11, 28 top, 65; Museo Arqueológico Provincial, Granada: 10, 30, 116; Museo Arqueológico Provincial, Sevilla: 52 left; Museo de Arqueología Nacional, Madrid: 22, 52 right, 80, 81 top, 87, 103 bottom, 112; Museo Nacional de Arte Hispanomusulmán, Alhambra, Granada: 37, 69, 71; Museu d'Art de Catalunya, Barcelona: 4, 24, 67 top, 70 top, 110, 111; Museum für Islamische Kunst, Berlin: 1, 78 top, 82, 92 top, 92 bottom, 113 top, 113 bottom; Museum of Art, Cleveland,

purchases from the J. H. Wade Fund: 15, 21, 29 top; Museum of Fine Arts, Boston: 32, 49, 77; National Maritime Museum, London: 98, 99; Spink & Son Ltd, London: 53 (now in the Davids collection, Copenhagen), 61, 81 bottom (now in a private collection, Kuwait); Victoria & Albert Museum, London: 20, 90, 107.

Werner Forman would also like to thank the following for their assistance:
Attmeol Ajjabi, Professor Martin Almagro Basch, Professor Klaus Brisch, Jan Fontein, Fernando Fernández Gomez, Amar Khelifa, Ursula Korneitchouk, Manuel Sánchez Mariana, Bashir Mohamed, Dr Barbara Mundt, Ricardo Olmos Romera, Larry Salmon, Hipolito Escolar Sobrino, Dr. Johannes Zik, Juan Zozaya.

INDEX

**Almoravid Empire
11th-12th centuries**

**Area of Almoravid Empire
conquered by Almohads**

**Almohad Empire
12th-13th centuries**

•Santiago de Compostela

A S T U R I A S

N A V A R R E

PYRENEES

Duero

Saragossa•

C A S T I L E

A R A G O N

P
O
R
T
U
G
A
L

Alcantara•

Tagus

•**Toledo**

Lisbon•

Badajoz

Guadiana

Valencia•

Merida•

Las Navas de Tolosa•

Denia•

Cordova•

Seville•

Guadalquivir

•**Jaen**

Murcia•

Cadiz•

SIERRA NEVADA

•**Granada**

Malaga•

Almeria•

Algeciras

Tangier•

Ceuta

Oued Sebou

**Rabat al-Fath
(Rabat)**•

Tlemcen•

Meknes•

•**Fes**

Oum-er-Rebia

Moulouya

Oued Tensift

Marrakesh•

•**Tinmel**

HIGH ATLAS

•**Sijilmasa**

Sous

Oued Dra

THE MUSLIM WEST

between the eleventh and thirteenth centuries AD